ACHIEVING ADULTHOOD

GERMAINE SMITH

THE CENTER FOR HEALING PRESS

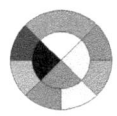

© 2016 by Germaine Smith. All rights reserved.

ISBN : 978-0-9960421-2-3 (print).
Library of Congress Control Number: 2016909700

Cover © The Center For Healing, created by Beth Mahutchin
Cover designed by Ann Delgehausen, Trio Bookworks
World Symbols © The Center For Healing, created by Paul Deziel
Medicine Wheel Symbol created by Mary Mohan.

All rights reserved. No portion of this publication may be reproduced or transmitted in any form or by any means, electronic or mechanical, including photocopying, recording, or capturing on any information storage and retrieval system, without permission in writing from the publisher, except by a reviewer who may quote brief passages in a critical article or review to be printed in a magazine or newspaper, or electronically transmitted on radio, television, or the Internet.

For reprint permission, email germ@thecenterforhealing.us.

The Center For Healing Press is the imprint of The Center For Healing,
a spirituality center of education and prayer for those seeking wholeness.
Contact: germ@thecenterforhealing.us.

DEDICATED
to all seekers, brave and fearless,
especially the next generations:

Emily and Connor
Mandy and Wade with Brynn
Tony and Ashley with Jordan, Kendra, Eli, Jenna, & Todd
Amy and Matt with Levi
Stacie and Phil with Alexis & Aaron
Corey and Brenda with Quinn & Evan
Steve and Jana with Annika

IN GRATITUDE
for all teachers, wise and inspiring,
especially mine:

Beth Mahutchin
Maria Bergeson
Byakuren Judith Ragir and Clouds In Water Zen Center
Semier Sycalli and Masjid El As-Salam
St. John's School of Theology and St. John's Abbey
Mount Zion Temple
Ned Mohan and Hindu Mandir of Minnesota

WITH ABOUNDING THANKS
to all who assisted, supporting and challenging,
especially:

Connor Blacksher
Mary McPherson
Mary Mohan

TABLE OF CONTENTS

0.	Seeking Adulthood	1
	The Journey	3
	Integration in Graphics	7
1.	Authentic Ground	17
	Philosophy of Grounding	19
	1st Fundamentals	23
	1st Practices	33
	1st Gifts	41
2.	Fearless Consciousness	43
	Philosophy of Consciousness	45
	2nd Fundamentals	51
	2nd Practices	59
	2nd Gifts	67
3.	Balancing Power	69
	Philosophy of Power	71
	3rd Fundamentals	81
	3rd Practices	85
	3rd Gifts	89
4.	Ruthless Compassion	91
	Philosophy of Compassion	93
	4th Fundamental	101
	4th Practices	111
	4th Gifts	119

5.	Truthful Communication	121
	Philosophy of Communication	123
	5th Fundamental	129
	5th Practices	137
	5th Gifts	143
6.	Clear Intuition	145
	Philosophy of Intuition	147
	6th Fundamentals	155
	6th Practices	165
	6th Gifts	171
7.	Complete Surrender	173
	Philosophy of Surrender	175
	7th Fundamentals	187
	7th Practices	193
	7th Gifts	199
8.	Achieving Adulthood	201
	Going Forth	203
	The Art of Reading Others	207
	The Gifts	211
	The Promises of Adulthood	213

0. SEEKING ADULTHOOD

THE JOURNEY

Welcome to the adventure.
Please know wherever you are in your journey
    you are right where you need to be.
We are all seekers on the path to a fuller life;
    just start where you are and move onward.

The effort of seeking adulthood, this journey to wholeness
    centers on just two questions:
    Who am I?   Why am I here?

These questions need to be investigated repeatedly throughout life.
We are creatures who long for self-discovery.
Each of us has lessons to learn
    and objectives to accomplish this lifetime.
To leave this life with either unfinished means
    not only do we leave work undone,
    but we are still responsible to complete it.

There is no escape.
Hence, "take as much time as you need
    and do things as fast as you can."[1]

Each person is called to adulthood.
However that is a difficult task because our culture
    teaches boys not to grow up and girls not to grow old.
This is a myth of falsehood and deception.
We are not to stay adolescents but to be fully alive adults.
This demands responsibility, accountability, and commitment.

Achieving adulthood is invigorating, complicated,
    and challenging work that demands commitment.
Remember you are always in charge of your learning and your life.
Fearlessness, courage, strength and authentic power
    are our birthright.
We may not feel these attributes fully but they are ours.

We are spiritual beings in human form.
We long for both understanding and relationship with the Divine
    whoever we define God to be.
To this adventure in self and Divine discovery
    we bring our bodies, minds, hearts, and souls.
Fundamentally life is about union and integration.
As we celebrate and honor our diversity,
    we rejoice and proclaim the truth
    that we are connected with the entire Universe.
Trust yourself and your path on this journey of self-discovery.
The job of each person is to discover who she/he is
    and why she/he is here.
If my words help, so be it; if they do not, so be it.
"Take what you like, leave the rest."[2]

It is tempting to focus on others
    and the direction they may need to go.

---

[1] Mary Palmer, Psychotherapy Sessions, St. Paul, MN, 1996-1998.
[2] AA motto

In Alcoholics Anonymous we call this 'taking another's inventory".
Concentrate on your own issues.
 Only you can do your own work
        and it is impossible to do another's work.
Your highest self knows your truth and your path for this life.
Therefore your soul will motivate you to be fully alive.
But the body gets scared and often chooses detours.
Don't let this reality lead to dualistic thinking
        that the body is "bad" and the soul is "good".
Adulthood is the integration and partnership
        of both aspects of humanity:
        honoring, listening, and developing both.
When I wrote a book on healing from abuse
        I chose the title: Between Lost & Found.
Someone asked me why I didn't entitle it From Lost to Found
        indicating I had journeyed through and indeed was found.
My response was that while that is what we strive for
        most of us, in this life, are not completely "found".
As an abuse survivor and a recovering addict, I am never cured
        only in the process of recovering of my wholeness.
The same lesson applies to achieving adulthood.
Adulthood is a lifetime effort.
Having had moments of being fully alive
        I try to stretch those moments into minutes
        then stretch the minutes into hours,
        and the hours into days
        until my life is one of adulthood.
But it is a continual effort of discovery and learning.
It helps to remember to focus on the journey, not the destination.
The goal is to seek spiritual progress, not spiritual perfection.[3]
The path of integration
Achieving adulthood demands, we embrace, claim, and develop
        our body, heart, mind, and soul.
Healing the chakras provides a formula for achieving adulthood.

"Chakra" is a Sanskrit word meaning "wheel" or "disk".
The system I teach is based on seven chakra energy centers
        that form a vertical column
        from the base of the spine to the crown of the head
        with each chakra numbered one through seven.[4]
These seven chakras of the human person work together as a whole
        and each has individual responsibilities.

Each specific chakra corresponds with an area of the physical body
        oversees emotional and sensory input and output
        governs specific areas of our mental being
        and connects to Earth and Divinity.
When a chakra is healthy, it is open and spins easily.
This means my energy is strong and useful for me.
When a chakra is compromised, it has some block
        and spins with difficulty.
This means I have energy that is unhealthy or not useful to me.
A compromised or blocked chakra holds any pattern of energy
        that is not helpful for me
        in my quest of achieving adulthood.

---

[3] Alcoholics Anymous, (New York City, NY: Alcoholics Anonymous World Services, 1976), 60.
[4] Judith Anodea, Wheels of Life, (St. Paul, MN: Llewellyn Worldwide, 1993), 1.

Energy is always in motion, in vibration.
When energy is stuck or blocked,
    all aspects of our health are jeopardized.
For example, when my fifth or throat chakra is compromised,
    the block will manifest itself in my energy field
        but also in my physical, emotional, mental,
            or spiritual self.
    I may develop a sore throat or feel unheard
    or have a propensity to silence my truth.
If I pay attention to my behaviors, feelings, thoughts, impulses,
    I can often learn which chakra is compromised.
On any given day,
    I probably have at least one chakra compromised.

On a difficult day, I have a lot compromised.
That's just reality—
    part of being human.
My job is
    1] to be aware one chakra is in difficulty
    2] work to heal and reopen it.
Of course, that is easier said than done.

Nevertheless, achieving adulthood requires that we learn
    to be sensitive to sensations, emotions,
    energy, thoughts, and behaviors.

This technique is often called "reading".
I call this "going inside" to listen to the inner world of energy.

Reading entails being still and being aware of the energy.
I can read my physical body, my emotional status, my spiritual state.
When you go inside yourself and listen,
    you may hear a voice   [Clairaudience]
    see a vision   [Clairvoyance]
    have a knowing in your gut   [Clairsentience]
    feel the energy of truth in your body.   [Kinesthetic]

You are not crazy or mentally ill you are not even abnormal.
You are doing what the human body was built to do:
    connect to the soul and the spiritual world.
Humans are, after all, mystical creatures.

One method is not better than another, just different.
Each person will have to identify what pathway works best
    and then she/he can work to develop it.
People working with energy have had many names in history:
    mystic, seer, dreamer, psychic, intuitive.
All are synonyms meaning one is sensitive to energy:
    energy of one's own body and soul, energy of others,
    energy of every part of creation, energy of the Universe.

All human persons are intuitive; mysticism is our birthright.
It's like having muscles—every person has muscle tissue
    but some develop theirs more than others.
Every one of us can learn to increase our sensitivity.
All it takes is practice.

Chakra work is the breadth and depth of integration
    for the human person:
        inviting symmetry of one's body, heart, mind, and soul;
        integrates the individual self with the whole of creation;

    and perpetual in its lessons,
        no matter one's age or abilities.

Sometimes the work is grueling and painful and painstakingly slow.
Sometimes the work is humorous and awe-inspiring.
Do your work as fast as you can but do not rush just to finish.
Wherever you are, honor the process of growth.
Blessings on your journey.

INTEGRATION IN GRAPHICS

The Sacred Weavings emblem on the front cover is based
    on the American Indian medicine wheel.
The inner circle of color represents the four areas of healing:
    yellow signifies the body, red is heart, black is mind,
      and white is spirit.

The outer circle of color represents the chakras:
    first chakra is red, second is orange, third is yellow,
    fourth is green, fifth is blue, sixth is indigo,
    and seventh is purple.

The Sacred Weavings emblem speaks to the need to integrate
    both the inner circle of body, heart, mind, soul
    with the power and integrity of the chakras
    in order to become fully alive.
As we heal ourselves, we heal the world.

The symbols used throughout this text
    were designed by Paul Deziel.
The pipe is important for American Indians
    a signal of peace and burns tobacco,
    the first gift of Mother Earth.

The lotus blossom grows out of the mud
    to become a beautiful flower.
This is an analogy of the human condition in Buddhism.

The crescent moon has a long history as an Islamic symbol
    centuries affixed on the roof of the Kabba
    Islam's holiest site in Mecca, Saudi Arabia.

For Christians, the letters "p" and "x" stand for "Pax Christi'
    the peace of Christ.

The Star of David is an ancient symbol of Judaism.

The eight-stoked wheel is the Hindu symbol
    reminding us that all paths lead to the Divine.

Chakras Embodied

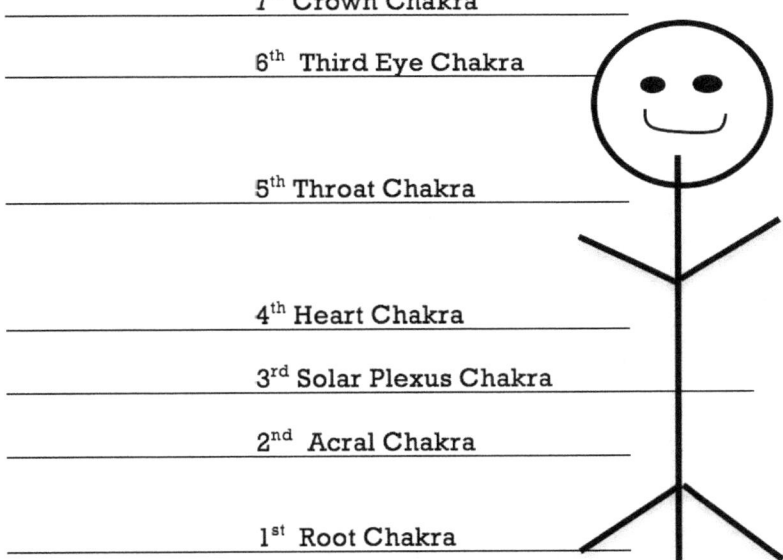

Chakra Overview[5]

CHAKRA	LOCATION	COLOR	GOVERNS
1	Bottom of the feet to base of tailbone	Red	Survival Laws of planet Abundance Dogma
2	Pelvis	Orange	Consciousness Creativity
3	Solar Plexus	Yellow	Power Will Habits Place in World
4	Shoulders Arms, hands, fingers Chest	Green	Relationships
5	Neck Throat Face Right eye	Blue	Communication
6	Third eye Left eye Skull	Indigo	Intuition Perception Vision
7	Crown of the head to 18" above head	Lavender	Connection to Divine

[5] Anodea, Wheels of Life, 60, 112, 166, 210, 258, 314.

Chakra Overview Continued

CHAKRA	RELATION	SOUND	VERB
1	With the Earth	Uh as in huh	I have
2	With emotion	O as in due	I feel
3	With immediate world	Ah as in father	I can
4	With greater world	Ay as in play	I love
5	With truth	Eee as in see	I speak
6	With Energy	Mmm as in Om	I see
7	With the Divine	Ngng as in sign	I know

Sacred Weavings Integration[6]

CHAKRA	RELIGION	CONNECT THROUGH	PATH
1	Indigenious People	Roots	Respect for Earth
2	Buddhism	Creativity	Fearlessness
3	Islam	Prayer	Practice
4	Christianity	Chords	Boundaries
5	Judiasm	Voice	Honesty
6	Hinduism	Vision	Inclusiveness
7	Personal Spirituality	Union	Trust

[6] Created by Beth Mahutchin and Germaine Smith.

Sacred Weavings Integration Continued

CHAKRA	"GOD" IS	PRAYER	GOAL
1	Mystery	Ground	Groundedness
2	Consciousness	Meditation	Consciousness
3	Union	Praise	Power
4	Love	Service	Compassion
5	I AM	Study	Communication
6	Truth	Contemplation	Intuition
7	One	Surrender	Wholeness of Adulthood

Chakras Compromised[7]

CHAKRA	BODY	HEART
1	Leg & knee issues Large intestine issues Obesity or anorexia Bone issues	Survival mode Abandonment issues Feeling empty
2	Genital issues Sexual issues Impotence & Frigidity Kidney & Bladder issues	Asexual or seductive Stubbornness Emotionally numb Emotionally excessive Feeling deprived Needy
3	Ulcers Stomach issues Diabetes	Aggressive or lethargic Defensive Feels powerless but acts domineering Abdicates responsibility Passive aggressive Poor self-esteem
4	Heart disease Lung disease Blood pressure issues Asthma	Lonely Critical & negative Judgemental Codependent Excessive loyalty
5	Neck & throat issues Mouth & teeth issues Colds Hearing issues	Mistrusting Fearful of truth Blaming Complaning
6	Vision issues Blindness Headaches Nightmares	Hyper Vigilant
7	Brain & skull issues Depression Boredom & apathy Alienation	Excessive self-reliance

---

[7] Anodea, Eastern Body, Western Mind, 82, 83, 138, 139, 204, 205, 264, 265, 314, 315.

Chakras Compromised Continued[8]

CHAKRA	MIND	SOUL
1	Scattered Panicked Entitlement Scarcity	Lost
2	Stagnant Stuck	Inert Unconnected
3	Controlling or yielding Always right or never right	Out of balance
4	Self-centered Egotistical Clingy	Abandoned Lonely
5	Exaggerates or lies Talks incessantly Shy	Non-communicative Only speaking Only listening
6	Image over reality Can't see alternatives Fantasizes	Spiritually blind
7	Value knowledge over Belief Rationale over faith	Cut off from the Divine

[8] Anodea, Eastern Body, Western Mind, 82, 83, 138, 139, 204, 205, 264, 265, 314, 315.

1. AUTHENTIC GROUND

PHILOSOPHY OF GROUNDING

Grounding is the state of being connected to the earth.
All creation is intrinsically, inherently part of this dirt we walk on
    his earth under our feet.
There is a tendency to stress one's connection to the Divine,
    not to the earth.
But without a healthy balance of both
    emphasizing the former may actually negate the latter.
The material and divine worlds act in collaboration.
This paradoxical dance of transcendence and eminence,
    of body and soul,
    is the art of being fully alive
    of walking a spiritual path in a physical body.[9]

Grounding necessitates the embrace of the body
    and the physical world as vital partners
    with the soul and the spiritual world.
Without this connection, human beings cannot become fully alive.

To be grounded and rooted is perhaps one of the most important
    and least recognized needs of the human soul.[10]
We are earth and She is our mother.
Not only do I depend on the earth for my survival, I am earth.
My body is earth elements of carbon, hydrogen, nitrogen, oxygen.
If I reject the earth, I reject myself.
When I treat the earth as an inferior aspect of grace
    I disallow the sanctity of my body.
Wholeness demands that I honor both
    body and soul as equally holy.

Grounding is the essential first step of spirituality.
We are fully in the core of our being
    our center point when we are grounded.
My therapist calls this being "plugged in"[11].

We are connected to the earth, plugged in to Mother Earth,
    know fully that we belong here
    embracing both our dignity and worth.
We know who we are.
There are only a few times when one should not ground
    because it too hard on the body.

When in shock from emotional or physical trauma
    grounding is not recommended.
After the crisis has past and the shock eliminated
    one can ground again.

The vast majority of time being grounded is the natural state
    for bodies and souls.
Without grounding
    we are unstable, thinking and acting faster and faster.
We may be a bit out of control, like a top off its axis.

---

[9] Mahutchin.
[10] Edward Sellner, Pilgrimage, (Notre Dame, IN: Sorin Books, 2006), 35.
[11] Denise Hanna Bisanz, Psychological Therapy Sessions, 2014.

We may think we are making great strides because of our speed
        when in fact we are only spinning in place.

Losing Ground/Finding Ground
I can spin a lot.
And for a long time I was not even aware of my spinning.
To increase my awareness,
        one of my teachers instructed me to pay attention
        to my emotions during the simple task   of grocery shopping.
I discovered that I would go to the store feeling relatively calm.
Afterwards however, I was anxious, hurried, and scattered.

My teacher's theory was that grocery stores provide us
        with the most basic human need —food—
        therefore there are many concerns for the shopper.[12]
Does this store have the items I need in stock?
How does one balance nutrition, economy, cravings, convenience?
Which is the fastest checkout lane?
Will there be enough money?
Should I buy extra in case the store runs out in the future?
All these legitimate questions tend to bring out fears
        and unground us.
In addition, everyone else in the store is asking the same questions,
        thus increasing the anxiety and spinning within the store.

Therefore, not only am I spinning and ungrounded,
        the atmosphere that I am in is spinning and ungrounded.
This lesson helped me to understand
        not only what spinning felt like—

        hyped up, anxious, fretful, speeding, and exhausted—
        but convinced me of the necessity for being grounded
        in order to be calm, in control of myself, and present.

Grounding gives us the balance of being anchored
        deep in the earth while ascending to the Divine.
When grounded, we know and appreciate our place in the world.

We're secure in ourselves and enjoy the clarity of our own identity.
The rest of the world may be in chaos, but I know who I am—
        this is my place in the world, and I belong here.

Being in a grounded state of attentive connection
        to the earth has many benefits.
It is the basis for understanding that authentic security
        comes from within, not from outside one's self.
When grounded I am "home"
        and only then can stand in my authenticity.

Being grounded allows us to have better boundaries.
        I can act, not react;
        I can respond without fear or panic.
Because we are anchored
        it is more difficult for others to manipulate us.
We can live in the present moment without anxiety or worry.

---

[12] Mahutchin.

Grounding and Surrender
The experience of being a fully alive human person demands
> we accept both the body and the soul
>> as integral partners in adulthood.

The greater my anchor into earth energy,
> the greater foundation I have to connect
>> to Divine energy.[13]

In other words,
> the more grounded I am, the more spiritual I can be.

While grounding is the first step of integrating the body and soul
> the recognition of and partnership with a Higher Power
>> also begin in the first chakra.

The essence of this partnership with the Divine is surrender.
Grounding and surrender are the bookends of our spiritual life.

Grounding brings our body and soul home
> connects the Earth and the Divine.

Surrender invites us to embrace the reality of the body and the soul:
> we are part of the Earth and part of the Divine
>> not the totality of either.

Together grounding and surrender teach us
> the humble dignity of who we truly are as human beings.

Surrender, described in chapter seven, begins in the first chakra
> with our acceptance of our limitations.

There are a host of distractions on our journey to wholeness:
> addictions, over-indulgences, neglect, abuse, violence, egotism, excessive pride, fear, guilt, resentment, greed, entitlement, self-righteousness, shame.

Surrender is the spiritual counter to distractions and temptations.
This does not mean giving up.
Surrender is the act of giving over the things in life we can't control.

As an addict, I have found great wisdom
> in the Twelve Steps of Alcoholics Anonymous.

It does not matter if you are an addict or not—
> in life we are all powerless.[14]

The first step is to admit our powerless.

In other words,
> no human power is in control of how the universe unfolds.

Every time we think we are in charge,
> our lives become unmanageable.

Then we came to believe a Power greater than ourselves
> could restore us to wholeness—
>> no matter what our woundedness or fullness,
>>> limitations or gifts.

Our wholeness, our completeness is woven into our acceptance
> of an Ultimate Reality that brings all that exists into union .

That belief invites the next step:
> a decision to turn our lives over to the care of the Divine.[15]

---

[13] Bergeson.
[14] Alcoholics Anonymous, 59.
[15] Alcoholics Anonymous, 59.

Groundedness and surrender are the tandems of our spiritual life.
Being grounded is the first step on our journey
        to being a fully alive human person
            and surrender is our ultimate conclusion.

1st FUNDAMENTALS

1st Chakra Basics

Location	From the bottoms of feet to the base of tailbone
Color	Red
Religion	Native American Indian and Indigenous peoples
Governs	1. Grounding
	2. Survival on all levels
	3. Laws of the planet
	4. Abundance levels
	5. Dogma and belief systems

1. Grounding

Grounding is the state of being connected to the earth.
It is the first step of all spiritual practices.
Therefore it is imperative that we connect to the earth.

One can ground anywhere, at any time.
I ground every morning as part of my morning prayer.
And often ground throughout the day, depending on my interactions.
Varieties of ways to ground are found in the 1st Practices section;
        play with the options.

As you practice grounding
        learn to identify when you are not grounded or centered.
Some clues grounding is lost:
        talking without listening
        talking too much
        moving or thinking faster and faster
        losing boundaries with others
        forgetting what you said or heard
        being manipulated or manipulating.

As soon as you realize you are ungrounded, ground and center yourself.
Gently analyze where and how you lost your groundedness.
Learn for the experience.

2. Survival On All Levels

Survival is fundamental and the foundation of health.
Physical well-being starts with the basics:
        food, shelter, safety, medical care, education, etc.
  Emotional survival means one knows that she or he has value
        and can successfully defend an attack of that value.
Spiritual health demands that we claim our own beliefs
        and our own connection to the Divine.
When the first chakra is healthy, survival is not an issue.
A compromised first chakra means on at least one level
        [physical, emotional, mental, spiritual]
        and maybe on all four, we are struggling to survive.

One's fundamental responsibility is to survival.
No species can grow well when it feels endangered.

If you are threatened in any area of your life
>   you absolutely need to protect yourself:
>   leave the situation, end the relationship,
>   get legal assistance, etc.

Do whatever it takes because your life is worth it.

3. Laws Of The Planet

Our planet has laws that oversee its activity.
Planetary rules may be disputed by humans but not changed.
Our best course of action is to accept and embrace them.

Indigenous peoples are the spiritual tradition
>   woven to the first chakra.

Their traditions are most connected to Mother Earth.
If we want to learn how to walk on the earth with respect,
>   Indigenous traditions are the best teachers.

The beliefs and practices included in this chapter are commonly
>   found in the Dakota and Ojibwe Nations of Minnesota.

A. Earth is a learning and teaching planet.
All elements of creation are our teacher.
I grew up in a very strict Catholic household
>   where everything was either "right" or "wrong".

There was no middle, no ambiguity.
Consequently, I cultivated searing and hurtful self- righteousness
>   because I thought I knew all the "right" answers.

It still is my most severe character defect.

This kind of intolerance hurt others around me and preventing me
>   from learning anything.

Removing the dualism of "right or wrong"
>   I can better accept others where they are at
>   and learn my lessons a bit easier.

B. We are responsible to the natural world:
>   accountable for our own individual beings
>   as well as the entire planet.

Because every single entity on this planet is connected
>   and interdependent
>   what we do affects more than just ourselves.

Many members in our culture, past and present,
>   do not accept this law.

The historical roots for some of its non-acceptance
>   are found in Genesis 1: 28.

"God said, be fruitful and multiple.
>   Fill the earth and subdue it,
>   have dominion over the fish of the sea, the birds of the air,
>   and all the living things that move on the earth."

Part of the reason our planet is in such crisis right now is because
>   we have interpreted this as a Divine mandate
>   to act in selfish interests without responsibility or
>   accountability for the rest of creation.

A better interpretation of the passage is that humankind is obligated
>   and required to assist creation, not abuse it.

The ramifications of our continued "domination" are crystal clear.

If we continue to refuse to accept this law, we will kill the planet.
> And ourselves.

C. Ours is a planet of incredible abundance.
There truly is nothing lacking for any part of creation.
There are also cycles of sharing
> sometimes I give, sometimes I receive.

Sharing applies to individuals, families, communities, and countries.
Because not everyone needs the same thing at the same time,
> sharing requires an open heart and attitude of trust
>> that one will be able to give and receive what one needs
>>> when one needs it.

D. Our planet is a creation-centered planet.
Everything on this planet is created, decays, and goes back to earth.
Nothing is dormant very long.
Therefore diversity and uniqueness are abundant in creation.

A creation centered planet means there is a cycle of life
> creating and destroying, building and returning to Earth.

Things are born, live, die.

Presently, our cultural attitude is to avoid or deny
> the reality of death.

Dying is the one and only thing that all creatures must do.
During our lifetimes,
> we have choices about various aspects of our lives.

But not death.
Death is the one absolute aspect of our existence:
We all will die.

Embracing this law of the planet leads to a fuller life.
Only when we accept our dying, can we really appreciate our life.

E. Learn from creation.
All creation has lessons for us
> if we choose to pay attention and learn.

Be especially observant of animals, plants, birds, fish, and reptiles.
They exhibit habit patterns that relay messages of healing
> and concepts of learning to anyone astute enough
>> to observe their lessons on how to live.[16]

Pay attention when they cross your path in the real world
> and in dreamtime.

They come with great teaching and further connect us to the earth.

For example, after a particularly difficult night of wrestling with fear,
> I ate breakfast in the porch of my Minneapolis home.

Standing in the street, not thirty feet from my front door, was a deer.
I stood astonished.
The deer just stood.

I knew the message immediately:
> deer symbolize the need to be gentle,
>> especially with one's self.

The deer brought me a message of both healing and learning.

There are multiple books and websites that explain animal totems.
When a creature crosses my path, I check several sources

---

[16] Jamie Sams and David Carson, Medicine Cards, (New York City, NY: St. Martin's Press, 1999), 13.

>to gather information regarding
>the animal's timely purpose.

F. Use nature's medicines.
Medicine is defined as "anything that brings
>personal power, strength, and understanding".[17]

Most religions use elements from nature in healing or ritual
>such as Christianity using water, oil in bread, and wine.

We relate to many aspects of natural elements:
>>the sensory components of seeing, hearing, smelling,
>>>tasting, touching;
>>the capability of physical elements with the spiritual;
>>the power of the element itself to heal.

Many Natives of Minnesota use four medicines:
>sage, cedar, Sweetgrass, and tobacco.

The herb sage is burned to help bring us back to our center.
Its smoke rises,
>clearing the space to renew positive spiritual energy.

Smudge to cleanse and purify, to replenish, and to heal.
Saging can also help us clear our own stale thoughts and actions
>in order to create an invitation or opening for new growth,
>>for positive experiences, and spiritual advancement.[18]

To use sage, light a small piece of sage and let the smoke rise.
Grab the smoke with the right hand
>bring it over the crown of the head.

Then bring the smoke down the front of the body to the ground
>and the back of the body to the ground.

Warning!
When sage is burned it can smell just like marijuana.
It won't get you high, has no addictive or hallucinogenic properties—
>it's function is to cleanse the space.

It just <u>smells</u> like pot.

When I was teaching "World Religions" at a Catholic high school
>>and introducing the students to sage
>>>folks would run into the principal's office
>>>>panicked we were smoking pot in the chapel.

Cedar tree leaves are used for cleansing and protection.

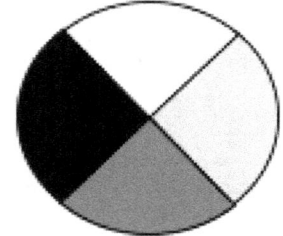

Purpose: service   Season: winter

WEST: black
Age: adult
Purpose: work
Season: fall

EAST: yellow
Age: birth
Purpose: beginnings
Season: spring

SOUTH: red   Age: adolescence
Purpose: growth   Season: summer

---

[17] Sams and Carson, 13.
[18] Michael Caduto, Everyday Herbs in Spiritual Life, (Woodstock, VT: Skylight Paths, 2007), 25.

When burned, cedar cleanses
>   particularly if energy has been thrown.

For example, if someone becomes verbally abusive
>   they are throwing energy in the form of words.

Burning cedar cleanses both the person and the space
>   from unwanted negativity.

To use cedar for protection
>   place some in shoes, medicine bag, or pocket
>   when anticipating a potentially dangerous
>   emotional, physical, or spiritual situation.

Sweetgrass is a prairie grass that when burned, heals
>   and strengthens the heart
>   especially a grieving or emotionally broken one.

Because it is considered Mother Earth's hair,
>   it is braided before it is burned.

Then it is lit and held in front of the heart
>   letting the smoke mend and restore.

Sweetgrass does not negate sorrow;
>   it lessens grief's duration and intensity.[19]

Tobacco is considered the first gift of the Earth.[20]
Hence it is used to give thanks back to both Mother Earth
>   and the Creator for all the gifts received.

Tobacco teaches us to be grateful
>   no matter what our situation may be.

You "puts out" tobacco by taking a small amount in your left hand.
State what you are grateful for, give heartfelt thanks,
>   and release the tobacco.

G. Karma exists.
Karma is a Sanskrit word meaning "action returned":
>   whatever I do comes back to me.

All religions believe this, though they all use different words.
Judaism, Christianity, and Islam speak of Divine justice,
>   that there is an reckoning for misdeeds that hurt others
>   as well as Divine blessings for deeds that heal the world.

Hinduism and Buddhism weave the word "karma"
>   with the concept of reincarnation.

Regardless of how one phrases it,
>   we are accountable for our actions.

There is no escape.

Karma means what I put out into the world returns to impact me.
One theory is that karma occurs on a one-to-one ration.
If I steal ten dollars, someone will steal ten dollars from me
>   in this lifetime or the next.

Another theory is that the ratio is one-to-three
If I steal ten dollars, someone will steal thirty from me.

The reason the karma is tripled in this theory
>   is because when I steal,

---

[19] Mahutchin.
[20] Mahutchin.

I steal a lot more than just the ten dollars.
I steal trust, security, sense of well-being, trust,
        effort and time to replace the money, etc.
So my karma must match the totality of what I stole.
This makes for a great motive to be honest in all my dealings.
It also invites me to be generous.
If I give someone ten dollars, I will receive thirty.

G. You have a path to walk this lifetime.
And you will walk off that path on occasion.[21]

Think of life like the veins of a leaf.

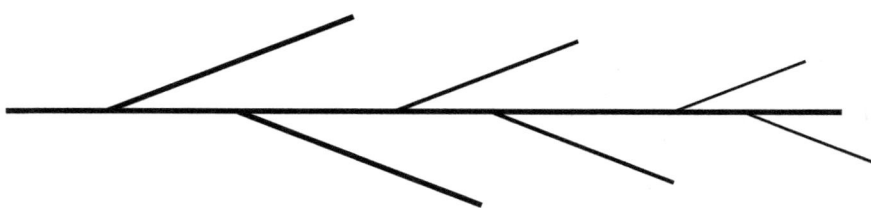

The Ojebwe call the walking of one's path
        "walking the good red road"
        and is symbolized as the main vein on the leaf.
Walking the good red road means I have a path
        a purpose to accomplish this lifetime.

But sometimes we get lost and step off our path.
When we are younger, the diversion off our path is long
        and it takes us a while to get back on track.
But as we mature, the detours off get shorter
        and the journey back quicker.

Examine your history and recognize times
        you ventured off your path.
If you notice you are off now, seek to return.

Be gentle.
You learned much while on your detour.
Take those lessons with you as you return to your authentic path.
You have purchased them
        through your time, efforts, struggles, and pain
        and those lessons are valuable as you journey forward.

H. The Medicine Wheel is the concept that life is circular
        and all of existence fits in the Wheel of Life.[22]

It is usually associated with the four directions:
        east, south, west, and north
Everything matters because everything is connected.[23]
All things in creation fit in the circle.
Humans are a part of this circle, not the controllers of it.
There is a harmony and natural flow in life
        an acceptance that life is unfolding as it should.

---

[21] Mahutchin.
[22] Blackwolf and Gina Jones, Listen to the Drum, (Salt Lake City, UT:L Commune-a-key Publishing, 1995), 70.
[23] Sams and Carson, 41.

Patience is an important element of grounding.

This means one waits
        one does not push to get the results one wants.
The practice of living life in a circle and not a straight line
        is the art of embracing the interconnectedness of all life
        is the gift of integrating the past, present, and future
        is the practice of being patient with self and the Universe.

4. Abundance Levels

Abundance is our attitude toward and our ability to
        claim possessions:
        physical items as well as beliefs and values.[24]

Abundance is about balance:
        not having more than we need
        not having less than we need.
When the first chakra is compromised regarding abundance levels,
        one is either seeking excessive acquisitions
        or choosing to be impoverished.
My sense of abundance is in balance when I believe and act
        with the attitude that all I need is available to me
        as I need it.

Remember needs and wants are different.
For example, I may want a newer car but I don't need one.
While it is essential to have a reliable vehicle for transportation,
        having one that is newest, fastest, or with more gadgets
        is a want—not a need.

That is not to say one should live a life of depriving oneself.
Abundance levels are out of balance
        when I act like I do not have enough when I indeed do.
Red flags are if I have to have more that I need,
        hoard or stockpile items because I fear scarcity,
        deprive myself out of fear, not reality.
This applies to any object of my desire.

The gift of living in abundance is
        asking for 100 % of what you want, 100 % of the time.[25]
And then letting go of trying to control the outcome.
Just ask and be open to receiving what is given.
As infants, others took care of our needs without our asking.
As adults, we are in charge of
        articulating our wants and needs to others.

The truth remains.
I am valuable. I have worth.
I have the right to ask for what I want and need
        with trust in the spirit of abundance.

5. Dogma And Belief Systems

Dogmas are philosophies, beliefs, or creeds we believe in.
Unhealthy or unhelpful dogmas are philosophies, beliefs, or creeds
        that we have accepted without question.
Being raised in a strict, authoritarian Catholic household

---

[24] Bergeson.
[25] Palmer.

I was taught being gay or lesbian was a mortal sin,
punishable by damnation in hell.

My unquestionably acceptance of this dogma led
  to sexual repression and hatred of my body and sexuality.

Blind obedience and unquestioning allegiance
  are not qualities of adulthood.

Dogmas are embedded in tailbone and legs of the first chakra.
Adulthood requires us to examine and investigate our dogmas.
Why do we believe what we believe?
Creating a belief system that embraces
  the interconnectedness of all creation allows
  for energy to flow more freely
  and open up the first chakra.

Changing the Pattern

The point of life is to be fully alive human persons.
To that end, we are always learning
  and learning forces us to grow, to change
    to integrate that new learning into our life.

Every chakra holds unhealthy patterns that will need to be changed.
While discussing change is in the abstract is very easy
  in real life it is difficult, frustrating, confounding, messy.

The change you seek may take days or years;
  it may upset the equilibrium in your relationships;
  it may take many relapses or multiple approaches;
  it may feel impossible.
But it is absolutely necessary.

Here are the basics of change:
A. Acknowledge that the behavior or attitude is not helpful to you

B. Put your intention on positive change.
Remember whatever you focus on grows
  so your intention needs to be affirming
  such as "I want to focus on recovery"
  rather than "I want to quit drugs."

C. Brainstorm possible changes that would be more helpful to you.
Most of us will do this as a mental activity;
  we can dream about various options and mew choices.
Work to attune your body and heart also.
How will you help your body when cravings begin?
What are healthier replacements for your old habit?
How will you handle temptation?
  Fear?   Panic?   Boredom?

D. Decide on the new action you think best for you.
Take small, manageable steps.

E. Evaluate.
What worked well?
What was difficult?

How do you need to handle setbacks?
Accept successes with gratitude.
Accept relapses as part of learning
FBe gentle.
This pattern you are breaking did not start overnight
        and most likely will not release overnight either.

Senior in my Space

When we are grounded, we are "senior in our space."[26]
Being "senior" means I understand and accept
        that I am fully responsible for myself in all my decisions.
Children are not capable of being senior in their space.
Between the ages of twelve and twenty-five, we learn to develop
        this action of being in charge and in control of our space—
        physical, emotional, mental, and spiritual.
As adults, no matter what our past, we are responsible for ourselves.

This "space" includes one's body and the personal space around it.
Referring to the grocery store example,
        I get spun out of my space
        when I go to a busy grocery store.
The energy in the store ranges from hurried to panicked to frenzied.

As soon as I leave the store,
        I can tell I have picked up energy that is not mine
        because I now am hurried or panicked or frenzied.

Being senior in my space means saying "No and Goodbye"
        with affinity to all energy not mine.[27]
To speak with affinity means I hold no ill feelings—
        no anger, no resentment—
        just compassion and neutrality.

While saying "No and Goodbye" to any energy is quite simple,
        getting energies to leave often challenging.
If I tell the energy to leave without affinity
        or without willingness let it go,
        it will come back and I will just reconnect to it.
Getting spun out or run by energy that is not mine demonstrates
        that on some level, I am agreeing to that energy.
This means I have some parts of my being
        where I am not choosing to be senior in my space
        but abdicating my responsibility
        and letting someone else be in charge.

Some hints for staying senior in your space are:
        Ground frequently.
        Be aware of losing your ground.
        Check your affinity.
        Are you harboring resentments?

When you say "No and goodbye" and the energy leaves
        there will be a void to fill.
Nature abhors a vacuum; that space must be filled.

Fill it with your own energy.
If you do not fill the space up with your own energy
        the old energy will return or another energy will enter.

---

[26] Bergeson.
[27] Bergeson.

This happened frequently to me
> when I was first learning how to be grounded.

I got spun out at the grocery store, came home, ground,
> and energetically cleaned my space
>> saying "no and goodbye" to energies I had picked up.

But after a few minutes, I would feel panicked and frantic again.
> I had forgotten to fill the space with myself.

Don't panic or berate yourself when you lose your seniority.
It is a very common part of being human.
Perhaps we were not taught how to be responsible for ourselves.
Perhaps that behavior was never modeled to us.
So we need to learn it now.
Like all practices, maintaining seniority is achieved through practice.
And all of us get lots of opportunities to practice.

1st Synopsis

When the first chakra is compromised, I lose my balance
> physically, emotionally, mentally, and spiritually.

I spin without connecting to anything.

Often acting in survival mode
> I don't feel the abundance of the Universe;
> then it is easier for me to abuse the planet
>> to get what I want.

Old, unquestioned dogmas overrule my present needs and beliefs.

When my first chakra is open and spinning well,
> I am connected to both the Earth and the Divine;
> my survival needs are met;
> I am attentive to the laws of the planet;
> I live in a spirt of abundance;
> and claim my belief system as my own.

I am home—body and soul.

1st PRACTICES

Grounding
From either a standing or seated position
>with your feet flat on the floor, comfortably apart
>>visualize the bottom of your feet.

See roots growing down into the ground from the arches of your feet.
Make your roots go deep into the earth,
>through the top soil, subsoil, earth's crust
>through granite layer, first fire layer,
>through conglomerate layer, second fire layer
>to the core of the earth.

[All sorts of energies collect in the first few feet of the earth.
If you ground into the top soil,
>you may pick up some other energy that you don't want.]

Draw up the earth's energy through your feet.
Bring it up your legs to the base of your tailbone.
Complete the circuit by dropping an imaginary cord into earth
>from your tailbone for the energy to drain back down.[28]

Qigong Grounding
Stand, with palms facing front of chest, out about 6-8 inches
Slowly, make circles
>bringing right palm in front left, from 3rd chakra to 5th.

Extend from 1st chakra to 6th chakra.
Stand with hands at chest, third fingers almost touching.
With each exhale, draw arms out to sides.
With each inhale, draw arms back to front of chest.

Other Grounding techniques

Lay down directly on the ground	Hug a tree
Use sweet grass or sage or cedar	Touch water
Put out tobacco in thanksgiving	Build a fire
Eat fruit	Regular exercise
Maintain regular sleep	Drink a glass of water
Take a bath	Gardening
Eat protein especially eggs	Smell flowers

If Your Grounding Isn't Working
Go inside your mind's eye and energetically sweep
>out the area beneath your feet.

Sweep from the bottoms of your feet to twenty inches into the earth.
Sometimes energies that collect on the earth's surface
>block our roots.

Place your intention on a clean, clear route to the earth's core.

---

[28] Bergeson.

Calling Your Soul Home
Our souls travel.
When we are grounded
        the soul resides a little above and behind the heart.[29]
It is important to connect the heart to the soul
        because we are souls taking a physical body.

Frequently the soul travels outside the body to work with others.
Fear, excitement, and prayer are other times the soul may travel
        outside the body.
We need to call ourselves home in order to be fully present.

Begin by saying your complete name
        and all the other names you use.
For example I would say, "Germaine Rae Smith…..Germ"
Picture yourself drawing your soul
        in through the crown of your head
            down through your skull, face, throat, chest, to the heart.

Wants and Needs List
Consider carefully the difference between wants and needs.
Make a wants and a needs list, listening to your body and soul.
How can you ensure you receive what you need?

Read the First Chakra
Go inside, to the mind's eye
        and read the strengths of the first chakra.

Read your feet.	What do you see? Hear? Feel? Know?
Read your ankles.	What do you see? Hear? Feel? Know?
Read your calves.	What do you see? Hear? Feel? Know?
Then the knees.	What do you see? Hear? Feel? Know?
Read your thighs.	What do you see? Hear? Feel? Know?
Then the base of tailbone.	What do you see? Hear? Feel? Know?

What are the strengths of your first chakra?
Examples might b: my knees are strong,
        I see my chakra sunk deep into the earth,
        my first chakra feels very balanced,
        my ankles are flexibly supportive.
Celebrate the strengths and power of your first chakra.

Go inside, to the mind's eye and read the blocks in the first chakra.

Read your feet.	Gleam lessons from your blocks.
Read your ankles.	Gleam lessons from your blocks.
Continue up the legs.	Gleam lessons from your blocks.
Read your calves.	Gleam lessons from your blocks.
Then the knees.	Gleam lessons from your blocks.
Read your thighs.	Gleam lessons from your blocks.
Read base of the tailbone.	Gleam lessons from your blocks.

What are the difficulties in your first chakra?
Examples might: my knees are wobbly,

[29] Bergeson.

I see my chakra hovering on the surface of the earth,
>   my first chakra feels very unbalanced,
>   my ankles appear distant from my legs.

Do you perceive any patterns?   Gleam lessons from them.

Is there one block you wish to choose to work on today?
Be gentle.
Everyone has blocks.
You can and will deal with yours.

Reading is an art, not a science.
Pay attention to your own style and manner of perception.
Keep a balanced outlook: celebrate the strengths of the chakra
>   and give thanks for the lessons the blocks present.

Remember this is about progress, not perfection.

Traditional Medicines
Practice with sage, cedar, sweetgrass, and tobacco.

Senior in Your Space
Where do you lose your seniority?
Do you detect any patterns
>   regarding where or with whom you lose your seniority?

Analyze your motives.
Are you remembering to fill the space with your own energy?

Receiving Unconditional Love Practice[30]
Ground and center yourself
Visualize your Higher Power
>   [Jesus, Allah, Yahweh, Mary, Ganesh, Buddha, Diana]
>   in front of you, bathing you in soft, shower of loving rays
>   covering every cell of your body from head to toe
>   covering every emotion, every strength, every wound

Be open to receiving this healing love
Trust this healing love over any distractions
>   or thoughts of unworthiness or doubt.

After several minutes;
>   join your Higher Power in an affirmation for yourself

Say "May I enjoy deepest wellbeing"
After several minutes, drop the visualization & and rest in the love

Changing the Pattern
1. Acknowledge that the behavior or attitude is not helpful to youm.
2. Brainstorm possible changes that would be more helpful to you.
    Listen to your body, heart, mind, and soul.
3. Decide on the new action you think best for you.
    Take small, manageable steps.
4. Evaluate.
    What worked well?
    What was difficult?
    Accept successes with gratitude.
    Accept relapses as part of learning.
5. Be gentle with yourself.
    Change takes time.

---

[30] Pema Chodron, Session Three 3,6, "Awakening Love", Jan 13 –Mar 6, 2011, audio tape, Sound Tunes, Gampo Abbey, Cape Breton, Nova Scotia, 2012.

Prayer to Mother Earth
O Mother Earth, ground me with your energy.
Fashion me, like You, to be creative and dynamic
    full of appreciation for my eclectic diversity,
    bursting with indomitable strength
    and embracing of my inherent beauty.

Lessons from Creation
Begin a habit of paying attention
    to what creatures crosses your path.
Look up what message they are bringing you.
What is your lesson?

Prayer to the Seven Directions[31]
To the Spirit of the East, the place of new beginnings;
    thedirection of the sunrise
    where hope is born and every day begins anew.
    Aho.   [Ojibwe word for "Amen"]
To the Spirit of the South, the place of growth and understanding
    the direction of warmth and rest and color and life. Aho.
To the Spirit of the West, the place of the ancestors
    the direction where adulthood takes wing
    and day comes to a rest Aho.
To the Spirit of the North, the place of dreams and vision
    the direction of service and Spirit
    where we listen and search for our life's path.   Aho.
To the Spirit of Mother Earth
    on whose back we walk upon, from which all life comes
    and to which all life must return. Aho.
To the Spirit of Father Sky, who gives life and breath to all. Aho.
To the God within, the sacred and holy part of me
    the soul that connects us to the heart that speaks truth.   Aho."

Medicine Wheel
Go inside and read your first chakra.
Where are you embracing the Circle of Life?
Where are you resisting?
How can you increase your vision of all of life unfolding as it should?

Read For Abundance Levels of Acceptance
Go inside and read for your acceptance that there is enough for all.
Do you believe you will receive what you need when you need it?
Do you possess an open hand, sharing what you have been given?
Are you caught up in hoarding out of fear that there is not enough?
Are you caught up in entitlement
    thinking you deserve more than others?

Go inside and read for your acceptance of the circle of life.
What are you birthing right now?
What are you releasing right now?
Are you birthing and releasing with gratitude?

---
[31] Palmer.

Go inside and read for your acceptance of the realities
> of life and death.

Do you appreciate your life, gifts and limitations?
Do you accept death as a part of life?
Have you discussed arrangements in case of accident or illness.

1st Chakra Meditation
Imagine a perfect physical environment
Place yourself in that environment.
For a few minutes, enjoy and be at one with yourself.
Open your senses—both physical & psychic.
> What do you perceive?
> Whatever is healthy for you there, draw it in.
> Whatever is unhealthy for you, say "no and goodbye" to it.

Know you can create this haven for yourself
Whenever you want or need it.

Read For Abundance Levels of Openness
Go inside your mind's eye and read for your openness
> and willingness to learn.

Where do you feel open?
Where do you feel constricted?
Where are you caught up in the dualism
> of "right or wrong" mentality?

Go inside and read for your needs.
Do you have what you need at this moment?
> If not, what do you need?

How can you ask or receive it in a healthy way?
If you do have what you need, are you grateful? Satisfied?
How much stuff do you have that you do not need or use anymore?
> Clothes, shoes, electronics, books, furnishings, etc.?
> Why? Examine your motives.

What is your fear if you let go of things you no longer need?
> How can you calm those fears?

Read For Dogmas
Go inside and read for dogma.
What religious beliefs do you hold as sacred?
> Where do these beliefs come from?

Are there exceptions to these beliefs?
> Why? Why not?

Where are your beliefs rigid?
> Why are these particular beliefs so unyielding?

Do you respect those who disagree with your beliefs?
Do you view those who disagree with you as wrong
> or as equal but different?

Where have you disagreed with your church/synagogue/ temple?
> Why do you disagree?

How did you feel when you challenged the religious authority?

Truth Barometer
Truth is what you believe or know to be genuine or honest.
Truthfulness is essential for walking a spiritual path.
Because we are so prone to deception, embellishment, and lying
        it is vital to embrace honesty as a way of life.
At the soul level, each person knows his or her own truth.
But humans struggle to be authentically honest.

Practice "knowing" truth.
One method is by paying attention to how it feels to speak the truth.
        What do you feel and where do you feel it?
Get a friend to listen to you or stand in front of a mirror
        then speak some truths.
Pay attention to the sometimes subtle shifts within the body.
Another method is to speak lies
        and pay attention to what you feel and where you feel it.
Again have a friend speak falsehoods to you
        or stand in front of a mirror, and speak some lies.
Practice listening to your truth barometer.
        Is there a difference between truths and lies?
        Do you feel them in the same way?
        Do you feel them in the same place in your body?

Grounding Morning Prayer
Stand with feet shoulder-width apart.
Keeping your back straight and bending the knees a bit,
        scoop up the air and the grounding energy from the earth.
Bring that air/energy up to your heart,
        keeping palms facing your body.

As your hands and arms reach your heart, turn the palms outward.
Continue to raise the arms as high as you can.
While keeping the elbows straight
        bring each arm down to its own side.
When your hands get to your hips, turn the palms toward the earth.
Push down with the palms toward the earth
        as if patting the ground, at hip level.
Ask Mother Earth to ground you.
You are part of Her. Ask Her for Her gifts today.
This is your place in the whole. You belong here.
This is your ground. You are meant to be here.
This is your place in the universe and it is good.

Run With the Animals[32]
Go inside and listen.
Be open to the four leggeds
        Which one comes to you?
        What message do they bring?
Be open to the winged ones?
        Which ones comes to you?
        What message do they bring?
Picture yourself being at the shores of the Pacific or Atlantic Ocean.
        What comes to you?
        What message do the waters bring?

---

[32] Bergeson.

Be with the rock people
> What rock formation comes to you?
> What message do they bring?

Put yourself somewhere your home state.
Where are you?
What is the message?
Let yourself go home.
Where are you?
What is the message?
Come back to present time, present place, present consciousness.
Listen attentively to all the messages received.
Invite in and embrace the Wise Mother and Wise Father energy
> of the created world

Know that all energies of the Universe are at your deposal.

Read for Surrender

Go inside and read for your willingness to surrender to the Divine
> whatever you conceive the Divine to be.

In what areas of your life are you powerless?
> Where do you struggle to admit powerlessness?
> Where is your life unmanageable?
> How does unmanageability manifest itself?

Do you believe there is a Power greater than you?
> Do you believe this Power can restore you to wholeness?

Are you willing to turn your life over to your Higher Power?
> Are you ready to surrender?

Mantras on the Gifts of the 1st Chakra

"Mantra" is a word or phrase that is repeated over and over
> to aid in focusing the mind.

Say the words slowly, either out loud or silently
> and let them rhythmically be on your breath.

Start with two minutes and gradually add time to your meditation.
There are three variations listed.
A. On the in-breath, say "I am connected";
> on the out-breath say "to Earth and Divine".

B. On the in-breath, say "I respect myself";
> on the out-breath say "I respect all creation".

C. On the in-breath, say "beauty;
> on the out-breath, say "beauty".

1st GIFTS

1. When I am connected to the earth
    and my soul is at home   I am grounded.[33]

2. When I understand the gifts of this planet
    are for all to share   I am abundance.

3. When I am senior in my space   I have a right
             to be here.

4. When I take responsibility
    for my life   I am security.

5. When I own my own beliefs
    and dogma   I am confidence.

6. When I work with all creation   I am interdependent.

7. When my body and soul
    connect in my heart   I am.

---

[33] Inspired by Megan Diamond.

2. FEARLESS CONSCIOUSNESS

PHILOSOPHY OF CONSCIOUSNESS

Consciousness is the art of being mindful.
It is the act of being fully alive, of being present in this moment—
    physically, emotionally, mentally, and spiritually.

Grounding is the integration and connection of body and soul.
It is only when I am grounded that I can be conscious.
The initial step in spirituality is grounding;
    consciousness is the conclusion.
The success, effectiveness, and morality of everything we do in life
    as well as the health of the rest of the chakras
    depends on our being grounded and conscious.

Consciousness is defined as awareness or perception.
This includes visual perception of my surroundings;
    emotional insights into my feelings
    mental awareness of my abstract thinking
    spiritual consciousness of human and Divine relationship.
All of this happens in the second chakra:
    being conscious of my present reality
      in the present moment

Hopefully we seek to increase our consciousness each day.
This means we strive to live in the present.
Living in the past or the future is easy
    and appears so v very attractive.
I hang onto yesterday's events out of regret, fear, or false security;
I can plan sorrow's events out of boredom, excitement, or control.
In reality I am avoiding the only real moment I have: the present.

Choosing to live in the present is so difficult in our culture
    because we are often tempted
      to deliberately choose unconsciousness.
Last week I had a fight with a friend.
I wanted her support and comfort; I got criticism and reproach.
Then I deliberately chose unconsciousness.

I ate too much, watched too much television, avoided any feelings,
    and vacillated between replaying our past conversation
    and creating a future conversation
      of telling her to go to hell.
In short, I choose to spin in the past and future
    avoid my present pain, and be unconscious.
Everything that makes us spin faster or feel more numb
    leads away from consciousness.
Our minds get programmed through repetition
    to go faster and faster, to jump from thought to thought.
This is called "monkey mind".
I think about one thing and
    unconsciously my mind bounces to another, then another,
    then another, like a monkey jumping from vine to vine,
      until I wonder how I got to my latest thought.
Because the sixth chakra [located at the forehead and skull]
    vibrates faster than the lower chakras,
      the mind has the ability to process thoughts very quickly.
But the human mind can only focus on one thought at a time.

It does not multi-task.
This indicates the mind is built for consciousness.
Its very construction provides an opportunity for me
        to focus on the solitary thought
           I am thinking at this moment.
Our task is to tame the mind,
        to reduce the unconscious thoughts
        and be mindful of the present.

This may sound boring.
After all, who wants to actually think about washing the dishes?
But if I am not mindful when doing mundane tasks,
        I will not be conscious during more important duties.

The Art of Self-Acceptance
Consciousness must be practiced.
It takes work because it is a state of being, not an event.
The goal is to live a conscious life, every second of every day
        not just during prayers in the morning
        or when we stop for a break.

One must be willing to face oneself in order to be conscious,
        to accept the gifts we have
        as well as the character defects.
Acknowledgement does not mean]
        we stop working to reduce our defects.
It means we do not deny the reality of our humanity
        at this moment in time.
Consciousness is achieved in small steps
        taken over and over and over.
This is because whatever we focus on grows.
What you concentrate on, you draw to yourself.

Therefore intention matters.
A difficult example is found in the USA's drug policy.

Since the USA government began its war on drugs,
        drug use has drastically increased in the United States.
Because what you focus on grows and the USA is focusing on drugs,
        drug use <u>has</u> to increase.

If the USA wished to end drug use in our society,
        we need to focus on recovery.
Then recovery, sobriety, and health would grow.

Consciousness is on a continuum.
One can always go deeper; there is always another level.
This should not discourage us but propel us forward.
The desire is always to be more conscious today than yesterday.

For example, I have had a lifetime of addictions.
In high school, I took drugs to numb myself and stay unconscious.
Then I switched to just alcohol.
Then after I began recovery from those addictions
        I focused on caffeine to help me avoid my demons.

I have learned there will always be something tempting me
        to avoid being conscious.
So having quit drugs, alcohol, and caffeine
        today I battle ice cream

My consciousness has deepened with each addiction I faced.
I still struggle but the struggle is easier because of my awareness.
Lessons I learned in recovery from drugs enlightens me
        in my other recoveries and in other areas of my life.

My Buddhist teacher gave a talk on
        "Finding Consciousness in the Pause"[34].
She referred to that moment when you move to the door
        to get out your numbing agent of choice—you pause.
Maybe for just a microsecond, but you pause.
This pause gives you time to make a conscious decision.
        What do I really need?

Consciousness is in the pause.
That is your moment to stop and be present
        to stop and break the pattern.
Her suggestion was to hold the pause for as long as possible.
        Then try to lengthen the pause... to stretch it out.
This allows you time to regain your consciousness,
        to ask yourself what step you really need to take.
The pause allows you to act in consciousness
        not react to temptation.
And consciousness allows you to make the best decision
        for yourself.

I know this works because for the first time in forty-five years
        I had the ice cream at the check-out counter
        I paused...
        and returned it to the freezer section.
Granted it took me forty-five years, but that is huge progress for me.

This is the great civil war that occurs within human beings.
The soul seeks to make great strides
        and the body reacts in trepidation.
Part of us wants to let go of bad habits
        part of us clings to them fiercely.
The task is to increase the pause—
        allow consciousness to permeate this moment
        calm the body and reassure the soul
        then make the best decision you can for today.

Remember to celebrate the successes
        no matter how small they may be.
It's always progress not perfection.

Cultivating Consciousness

Being conscious permits us to see life as it really is: as a paradox.
All life is a paradox.
Our job is to dance with the paradox rather than fight it.

Life's paradoxes include:
        human beings are both human and divine;

---

[34] Judith Ragir, Meditation Talk, (Clouds In Water Zen Center, St. Paul, MN) June 1997.

        we are all wounded and whole at the same time;
        all creation is both in development and perfect;
        hell and heaven are both right here on earth;
        I am an individual and a communal creation.

Buddhism is the best at teaching how to achieve consciousness—
        that is the goal of Buddhism.
To that end, Buddhists offer the gift of meditation.

Meditation is an excellent method of cultivating consciousness.
It is the art of self-acceptance through the practice of sitting still.
One sits on a cushion,
        welcoming the opportunity to consciously love one's self.
It is a practice of transformation, of truly accepting who we are.

Most of us live in our heads: analyzing, worrying,
        thinking, plodding.
Meditation strives to quiet our cerebral activity in order to listen.
Our common human need and spiritual requirement
        is to be still and listen.

I attended a lecture on the monastic history of Benedict of Nursia,
        who spent three years in a cave.
Abbot John asked, "Who do you bring into the cave with you?"
After a short pause, he answered,
        "Just yourself and all your demons.
        They all go with you into the cave."[35]

That is the point of the cave—
        to have the time and a place to wrestle with your demons.
There are no caves in my world
        but the meditation cushion serves the same purpose.
In meditation, it's just me — alone with my demons.

It is the time to truly face myself.
As I sit, my fears, resentments, worries, ego, selfishness
        —all my demons — will surface
        providing me an opportunity to deal with those parts
        of myself I often try to avoid.

We all have demons, shortcomings, and character defects.
But those parts of ourselves we judge as inadequate
        can teach us much if we are open.
They can provide the motivation to deeper awareness.
That is the point of meditation—
        to get to know, accept, and love all aspects of yourself.

Meditation helps one to: slow down;
        live in the present moment;
        reduces time spent worrying about the past or planning the future;
        permits one to authentically listen to the body
            without the mind's commentary;
        allows us the opportunity to feel what we need to feel;
        face our discomforts instead of denying or ignoring them;
        increase consciousness about our intentions;
        create and participate in one's life
            rather than passively observe.
In short, meditation invites consciousness.

---

[35] Abbot John Klassen, Lecture on Monastic History, (St. John's University, Collegeville, MN), April 8, 2010.

Meditation has been a struggle for me.
I understood the benefits but just could not sit and be still.
I played with many different avenues of meditation practice
        before I was able to meditate with any regular success.

So if you are new to meditation, be gentle.
Start with a manageable time, perhaps two to five minutes.
        [I started with two!]
Be tender with frustrations and recriminations.
Your demons will present themselves and your issues.
Deal with what comes up—
        whether physical, emotional, or spiritual—
        and attend to its healing.

For example, when I first starting sitting, I could only do two minutes
        because my pain would overwhelm me.
I started to attend to its healing by just acknowledging it
        admitting its presence.
The more I learned to accept my pain, the less hold it had on me
        and the longer I could sit in meditation.
Consciousness is the objective of adulthood.
Only when I am living a conscious life, am I fully alive.

2nd FUNDAMENTALS

2nd Chakra Basics

Location	Bottom of the tail bone to top of the hip
	Pelvis
	Genitals
Color	Orange
Religion	Buddhism
Governs	1. Being conscious
	2. Creativity in all forms
	3. Physical growth and cultural training
	4. Authenticity
	5. Emotional health

1. Being Conscious

Consciousness is essential for adulthood.
It is the state of being fully awake and mindful of one's self
    and one's surroundings.
Being conscious means we are fully present
    body and soul, in the moment.
The body is grounded; the soul is at home in the heart chakra;
    we are senior in our space, able to walk in wholeness.

2. Creativity In All Forms

The second chakra's great gift is creativity in all forms.
This includes sexuality, of course,
    as sexuality is one form of creativity.
Building new relationships or new business ventures,
    the arts, dance, poetry, literature, and music,
    theater, drama, imagination, and fantasy,
    home decorating, cooking, and apparel,
    building, engineering, constructing, and remodeling—
are just some of the aspects of creativity.

Creativity is finite energy so it must be regenerated.
Blocks to regenerating our creativity include:

being ungrounded	unconnected to the Divine
physically tired	emotionally stressed
mentally drained	spiritually unbalanced

Once I deal with the blocks to regenerating creative energy
    I have the opportunity to create what I want and need.

Sexuality is one of the most powerful
    and least understood aspects of our humanity.
As sexual beings,
    we are intrigued by our sexual nature and passions
    but also embarrassed and scared of them.
Adulthood means we seek to understand
    and claim our sexual selves
    through ethical behavior and education.

There are a plethora of sexual morals one can claim,
    from abstinence to friends
      with benefits to random hookups.

I favor a simple sexual ethic
      that demands conscious reflection and commitment.
My sexual code is:
      healthy sexual behavior is feeling and acting in a manner
      that corresponds to my highest truth.
This means I cannot participate in any activity
    that abuses myself or another.

Whatever your sexual code is, it is important to examine its dogma.
    Is this your code or someone else's?
    Does it lead to your highest truth?

The second facet of being a sexually mature adult is education.
Adulthood means we are courageously painstaking in our quest
    to ask and find the answers to our sexual questions.
Whatever your questions are, seek opportunities to discuss them.

3. Physical Growth And Cultural Training

The second chakra governs our physical growth
    and cultural training.
Whereas the aspect of physical growth is fairly apparent
    cultural training may be more murky.
It refers to all messages we receive regarding who we are
      and how we are expected to engage in the greater world.
Cultural training covers a multitude of areas:
    from attire to manners to career choice,
    from dating expectations to family traditions
      to gender identity.

If you were raised in a relatively functional family,
    your cultural training is probably healthy.
You are free as an adult to choose your family's cultural training
    and you know you will still be accepted
      if you do not choose it.
If you are from a family with more dysfunction,
      the expectation is high that you buy into
        all the cultural training
        and in challenging this training,
      you may not be supported.

An easy example from my family is the message of image.
During my adolescence my mother and I often argued
    about my attire.
My mother's choice of clothing for me was dresses and sweaters.
As a gay dike, I wanted to wear jeans, sweats, and tee shirts.
My mother wanted me to look feminine; I wanted to be butch.
My family had a traditional image of what it meant to be a girl
    that I did not fit at all.
It took me many years to unplug my cultural training
    in order to be myself
      not only in my attire but in my sexuality.
Examining the messages of cultural training received in childhood
    is a necessity in helping us to further understand
      both our acceptance and rejection of our unique selves.

4. Authenticity

Adulthood demands we take full responsibility
        for creating unique selves
            personally as well as professionally.
This is the source of authenticity—
        to claim our unique and genuine identity.
Being fake leaves us unfulfilled and serves no helpful purpose.

The power of this chakra is its focus on the positive "I can".
Scrutinize your self-talk language; eliminate any sentiment of "can't"
        the second chakra always moves us forward
        with confidence.
A crucial ingredient for us to stand in our authenticity is strength.
Strength is the universal energy that promotes life and wholeness.
It is constructive energy
        empowering us to be who we are intended to be
        leading us to be in action rather than reaction.

Cultivate increasing your awareness of when you need strength
        and be willing to ask the Divine for strength
        throughout every chakra.
Nurture the openness to receiving strength by visualizing it
        in all aspects of your being.

Conscious interdependency is mindfully creating relationships
        where each person involved can be whole.
One of the hardest lessons of adulthood is being aware of
        others' emotions but not taking responsible for them.

Some common evidence we have blocks in the second chakra:
        allowing another to control you,
        placating another's feelings,
        permitting others or some other outside entity
        to dictate the rules regarding emotions or sexuality,
        denying our creativity at home or work,
        feeling responsible for another's emotions,
        trying to "fix" or take care of another
            rather than taking care of yourself.

Conscious interdependency requires us to set
        appropriate boundaries to ensure our own authenticity.
We trust that others will be present to support and assist us,
        and support and assist others
        in their quest for authenticity.

This interdependency includes the act of creating.
It is in the second chakra that we create with others:
        friendships, business ventures, and children.
The success of both ourselves and our creations
        depend on our healthy interrelationships.

5. Emotional Health

While the first chakra deals with survival issues,
  the second chakra oversees emotional health.
Emotions are present in all chakras.
When emotions are out of balance
  the issue usually starts in the second.
The key to emotional health is our ability
  to recognize and acknowledge how we feel
  and recognize and acknowledge
    how another's emotions impact us.

Emotions are just energy—none are good or bad; they just are.
We try to assign a value to them usually based on what we want.
But at their essence
  emotions are just energy we need to feel and express.
While the second chakra governs our emotions,
  they are expressed and conveyed
  throughout all the chakras.

For example, codependency is described as unhealthy interplay
  between ourselves and others.
We don't have good boundaries
  therefore we surrender our sense of self.
Codependency resides in the fourth chakra.
But the emotional blocks that craft codependency
  start in the second.
Emotions are stored in the cells of the body.
When the second chakra is open,
  I become aware of the emotions
  surrounding a particular event.
I feel those emotional sensations in my body
  and express them in a healthy manner.
When I have dealt positively with them and learn any lessons
  they have for me,
  the emotions dissipate.
When I refuse to acknowledge my emotions, deny, or bury them
  they often get expressed in a manner that is harmful
  or even dangerous for me.
Although any emotion can be out-of-balance,
  some are perennially more challenging.
When in excess, they cause us great problems.

A. Fear is the perception that danger is imminent.
It motivates us more than any other emotion.

Fear has many names—
  panic, anxiety, worry, dread, fright, distress, terror—
  but all produce the same result: unconsciousness.

Permeating all my chakras I demonstrate fear
  in very unhelpful behaviors.
When I am afraid, I am ungrounded;
  I am paralyzed, frozen in my second charka;
  my heart closes;
  I either surrender my power or act too aggressive;
  my voice betrays me
    by either being mute when I need to speak
    or speaking too much when I need to be silent;

        I lose touch with my intuition in my sixth chakra;
        I feel lost, alone, and unconnected to the Divine.

Fear is a panic regarding an event we believe
        might happen in the future
        with its tentacles firmly rooted in the past.

For example, if I am anxious about a medical exam next week
        that event is in the future
        but my fear is triggered by my sister's death from cancer.
As a result, I am avoid going to the exam
        or spend hours worrying about it,
        or fib about my symptoms when I get there.
None of these options are heathy for me.

Because fear is such a motivator,
        it is imperative we examine our fears
        to discover the triggers from the past.
Only then can we make conscious decisions
        regarding our response to fear.

B. Pain is the communication that something is not right with us.
Physical pain is a signal something is infected, worn-out, or broken.
Emotional pain is the indicator that we have lost something of value.

As humans, we think avoiding pain is the solution to the problem
        when the pain is only a symptom of it.
This leads to denying our pain to evade the reality that we hurt.

C. Anger is a normal, healthy, very human emotion
        that occurs when we perceive we have been mistreated.
It requires expression in a manner
        that does not hurt one's self or any part of creation.

When we bury anger, it often comes out sideways—
        at the wrong person,
        at the wrong time,
        in the wrong manner.
For example, I would get angry at my boss
        so I would yell at my students,
        or road rage at the driver in front of me,
        or be antagonistic with the person at the checkout.

We do not teach our children how to deal with their anger.
        probably because we don't deal with our own anger.
Facing our anger requires two steps.
The first is to realize anger is always a secondary emotion.
There are always two other emotions behind our anger:
        pain and loss.
When I can look behind my anger,
        I am mad because I am filled with pain.
I lost something I desired and the greater the loss,
        the greater my anger.

If I stuff my anger
        I am really stuffing three emotions: fear, pain, and loss.
And they always become unstuffed sooner or later.

The second step in dealing with anger is to express it constructively.
There are many ways to learn how to express anger positively.
        Play with some of them to practice constructive anger.
For example, when I get mad at my boss,
        I often need to step away from the situation to figure out
        exactly what I am angry about
        and examine the pain and loss behind my anger.

This may take me awhile to process:
        I may need to talk with an objective third party;
        I may have to hit my punching bag.
Once I know what the pain and loss are,
        then I can decide what to do.

Perhaps I need to constructively express my anger to my boss;
        perhaps my pain has nothing to do with her
        and I can release my anger at her without discussion.
Regardless of the cause of my anger and pain, I need to face it.

D. Grief is the aching we feel at a loss.
It is real suffering that demands attention in order to be healed.
Never a sign of weakness,
        grief is a testament to one's ability to love.

E. Resentment is lingering bitterness after a disappointment.
It is the inability to let go of our pain or grief
        which then becomes toxic and spreads like poison.
Resentment hardens the heart
        cultivates sullenness, blame, and victimhood.
It is dangerous because it engenders hate.

F. Loneliness is the feeling that one is isolated
        from a meaningful connection to another.
It is a serious sensation of being all alone, abandoned,
        ignored, unloved.
I believe loneliness is the most unspoken emotion—
        no one wants to admit they feel unconnected or unloved.
That makes this emotion very perilous.
It can lead to depression, aggression, and further withdrawal.

Naming our loneliness is the first step to dealing with it.
I have been lonely most of my life
Growing up in an abusive home taught me to be secretive.

Drug addiction promoted unauthentic behavior and relationships;
        a strong introverted personality drew me inward.
I still work hard to overcome my feelings of separateness
        and isolation.
Like all emotions once admitted
        loneliness is not so overpowering and more manageable.

G. Pleasure is the sensation of enjoyment.
It is the emotion that comes when we get what we want or need.
Pleasure is the state we seek
        we want to be happy, content, and full of joy.

However one must be conscious of motives and consequences.
Acting out of pleasure can lead to self-indulgent egotism.

It is easier, not healthier to gravitate toward
        what brings me pleasure
        and avoid what brings me pain.

Nor is it mature to increase my pleasure at someone else's pain.
That is not the goal of adulthood
        but a childhood developmental stage
        based on reward and punishment.

Adulthood is fearlessly acting out of what is our highest good
        seeking wholeness in the midst of pain or pleasure
        but not motivated by either.

The formula to deal with emotions is easy to type out on paper
        yet incredible challenging to accomplish in daily life.

Regardless, all emotion must be:
    1] named and acknowledged;
    2] expressed in a healthy way.

H. Humor
Humor is the best tool for breaking up energy.
It can shift depression, deflate aggression, and intensify joy.

Each chakra center has its own type of humor.[36]
1st chakra humor centers on survival issues or slapstick comedy.
2nd chakra humor relates to creation and sex.
3rd chakra humor is odd humor, like when things don't fit.
4th chakra humor centers on relationships, dating, marriage, family.
5th chakra humor caters to words and language
        including "dry" or wry humor.

6th chakra humor is philosophical and abstract.
        Myths fit this chakra.
7th chakra humor centers on spiritual and afterlife topics.

The more a story touches a chakra center, the funnier it is.
Humor is excellent at breaking up energy.

However, when humor is misused, it can be divisive.
Sometimes, we say something we think will be funny but it is not.
        It comes out sharp or loud or too much.
Sometimes, we use humor to speak the truth
        but the joke is packed with barbs.
It comes out as a joke but embarrassing or accusatory.
Sometimes our humor is mean-spirited.
        We want to inflict pain with our joke.
For these occasions, apologize and analyze your behavior
        What is the root emotion behind your harsh humor?

---

[36] Bergeson.

2nd Synopsis
When the second chakra is compromised, I am not in a fully conscious state.
Red flags are:
>thinking or acting faster and faster;
> panic and anxiety;
>when my emotions are running me
>>rather than I handling my emotions;
>
>I react rather than respond;
>if I have no memory of an event.

The second chakra relishes authentic creativity and creative authenticity.
When this chakra is balanced
>I am living in a state of greater consciousness.

I create the life I want and need to have.
I can generate a healthy body, heart, mind, and soul.
I stand in my authenticity and encourage authenticity in others.

Embracing emotional health, I am able to feel my emotions
>and express them in ways that honor myself and others.

I have empathy for others.

2nd PRACTICES

Read the Second Chakra
Read the strengths of the second chakra.
Read your hips.   What do you see? Hear? Feel? Know?
Read your pelvis.   What do you see? Hear? Feel? Know?
Read your genitals.   What do you see? Hear? Feel? Know?
What are the strengths of your second chakra?
    Celebrate the strengths and power of your second chakra

Read the blocks in the second chakra.
Read your hips.   Gleam lessons from your blocks.
Read your pelvis.   Gleam lessons from your blocks.
Read your genitals.   Gleam lessons from your blocks.
Do you perceive any patterns?   Gleam any lessons..

Read the Emotions
Read your emotional health.
What emotions are present today?
    Are there emotions that are absent?
    Which emotions are in excess?
Are there emotional blocks?
Examine your motives for these blocks.
    How can you remove the blocks?

Sitting Meditation
Sit on a zafu [meditation pillow] or a chair.
If on a zafu, sit cross-legged, half, or full lotus.
When possible, one's buttocks and two knees support the body.
If on a chair, sit on the front third of the seat,
    with feet flat on the floor.
Keep the back and neck straight
    the nose on an imaginary line with the navel.
Place the hands at waist level or just below
    resting the back of one hand in the palm of the other
    with thumbs barely touching.
Rest the tongue against the upper front teeth at the gum line.
Let the eyes be soft, either partially or fully closed.
Maintain focus on the breath
    breathing in through the nose, out through the mouth.
If your mind wanders, bring the focus back to your breath.

Breath Meditation
Sit. On every in-breath, breathe in "Let God".
On every out-breath, breathe out "Let go".

Lengthen the Pause
Identify how and where you "stuff" your issues.
Look for a place to "pause".
Maybe it's just as you touch the refrigerator door;

maybe it's just before you grab the car keys.
Within that pause, consciously be willing to stop.
Put your intention on stretching out that pause
> holding it for as long as you can.

Walking Meditation
This meditation is to be walked as slowly as possible
> to aid the mind in slowing down.

Walk clockwise.
Hold your hands at the navel
> the back of one hand in the palm of the other.

Keep the back and neck straight
> the nose on an imaginary line with the navel.

As you lift your right foot, shift your weight to the left foot and leg.
Place the toes of your right foot on the ground first
> then the middle of the foot
> > and finally, place the right heel on the ground.

Slowly, shift your weight to the right foot.
Repeat for the left foot.

Read for Creativity
Read your creativity.
> How does your creativity express itself?
> What aspects of creativity arouse your passion?

Read for blocks in creativity.
> Where is your talent undeveloped or underdeveloped?
> What fears keep you from realizing your creativity?

Word Meditation
Choose positive or sacred words or phrases to direct concentration.
There are endless possibilities so play with different words.
Try a sacred person's name
> such as Mary, Krishna, Allah, Ganesh, Diana, or Adonai.

Try a characteristic or virtue you need
> such as trust, surrender, courage, strength, or peace.

Humor
Tell jokes to someone.
Laugh!

Steps in Creating
1. Be grounded and conscious.
2. Identify all aspects of what you want or need.
   > What exactly do you want to create?   Be specific.
   > When do you want to receive this creation?
   > How would you like NOT to receive it?
   > For example, you want a down payment for a house
   > > but you do not want to get the money
   > > > because someone dies.
   >
   > What do you need to do to create it?

How does it heal the earth?
3. Place your vision in an imaginary bubble.
4. Release it to the Divine.
5. Be patient.
    Trust the Universe is working for your greatest good.
6. Receive your creation with gratitude.

If you are co-creating with another person,
    both must strongly agree in the second chakra.

Vision Board[37]
[Items needed: manila file folders, pens, markers, magazines]
This is an exercise for creating a vision.
A. Spend some time listening to your higher self in meditation.
    Be open to Divine inspiration and partnership.
    Ponder what you desire to create.
    Consider the who, what, where, when, how of this creation.
    Consider how you do not wish to achieve this vision.
    Be as concrete and precise as possible.
B. On the manila file folder
    draw or cut out pictures that speak to your vision.
Use whatever artistic/design means you wish
    to visualize your vision.
C. When completed
    offer a prayer to release your vision to the Divine.
    Trust the Universe to provide what you want and need.
    Stand the manila folder up as a testimony to your vision.

Read for Sexual Health
Go inside and read your sexual nature.
    Is this your code or someone else's?
    Does it lead to your highest truth?

What are the strengths of your sexuality?
What blocks are present regarding your sexuality?
    What is the origin of these blocks?
What emotions arise when you face your sexual nature?
    What is the source of these emotions?

If you have been abused
    pay particular attention to blocks in your second chakra
When another's energy and behavior violated your sanctity
    you can restore yourself to sexual health and wholeness.
Reach out for help; reclaim yourself.
Recovering your wholeness is attainable.

Picture Meditation
Find or create a picture to aid in your meditation.
There are many options, so find what works for you:
    scenic nature scene, religious icon of a person or place,
    Mandela [Buddhist or Hindu geometric design].
As you sit, draw your awareness inward to the picture.
Practice being still, open, aware, and listening.

---

[37] Deana Downs, The Art of Self-Care Healing Session, October 2014.

Read for Cultural Training
Read for the information you received from family, teams, clubs
       regarding how to be in the world.

Reading for Consciousness
Read your present state of consciousness.
       Are you present in your physical body?
       Is your soul in your body?
       Do you sense squelched energy anywhere?

Receiving Word Meditation
Each day of the month, concentrate on a different characteristic
       that you wish to increase in your life.
For example, on January 1, be open to receive acceptance.
Using a string of beads, meditate on a particular word
       as you count off the beads with your fingers.
I chose to use the 108 beads of Hinduism
       108 symbolizing the entire universe.
Use the word for your sitting meditation
       then use it throughout the day to center yourself.
For example, use the word as part of your prayer before meals
       or when you are waiting at the stoplights
       or if you are early for a meeting and need to wait.

DATE/LETTER		POSSIBLE CHOICES		
1	A	Acceptance	Authenticity	Awe
2	B	Boldness	Beauty	Bliss
3	C	Commitment	Courage	Calm
4	D	Dignity	Dedication	Daring
5	E	Enlightenment	Earthliness	Essence
6	F	Fortitude	Forgiveness	Faith
7	G	Gentleness	Generosity	Gratitude
8	H	Health	Happiness	Honesty
9	I	Interdependence	Impermanence	Integrity
10	J	Joy	Justice	Join
11	K	Kindness	Kindle	Key
12	L	Love	Limitlessness	Luster
13	M	Mindfulness	Majesty	Mercy
14	N	Natural	Nurture	Noble
15	O	Optimism	Originality	Origin
16	P	Patience	Positivity	Power
17	Q	Quality	Quintessence	Quiet
18	R	Reliance	Rejuvenation	Resolve
19	S	Stillness	Strength	Splendor
20	T	Truth	Temperance	Trust
21	U	Universal	Ultimate	Unity
22	V	Vibrancy	Venerable	Valor
23	W	Worth	Wonder	Weave
24	X	Xenodochial	Xenial	X
25	Y	Yin/Yang	Yen	Yield
26	Z	Zenith	Zeal	Zappy
27	all enduring abuse	Fearlessness	Healing	
28	all suffering depression	Balance	Hope	
29	all caught in addiction	Recovery	Sobriety	
30	all preparing for death	Openness	Light	

Sending Word Meditation

Each day of the month, concentrate on a different characteristic
    that you wish to send to the world.
Offer your merit for everything in creation
    beginning with that letter.
For example, on January 1, offer acceptance
    to everything that begins with the letter "A".
Using a string of beads, meditate on a particular word
    as you count off the beads with your fingers.
I chose to use the 108 beads of Hinduism
    108 symbolizing the entire universe.

Use the word for your sitting meditation and
    use it throughout the day to send affirmations to the world.
For example, use the word when anger or impatience or fear arise.

DATE/LETTER		POSSIBLE	CHOICES	
1	A	Acceptance	Authenticity	Awe
2	B	Boldness	Beauty	Bliss
3	C	Commitment	Courage	Calm
4	D	Dignity	Dedication	Daring
5	E	Enlightenment	Earthliness	Essence
6	F	Fortitude	Forgiveness	Faith
7	G	Gentleness	Generosity	Gratitude
8	H	Health	Happiness	Honesty
9	I	Interdependence	Impermanence	Integrity
10	J	Joy	Justice	Join
11	K	Kindness	Kindle	Key
12	L	Love	Limitlessness	Luster
13	M	Mindfulness	Majesty	Mercy
14	N	Natural	Nurture	Noble
15	O	Optimism	Originality	Origin
16	P	Patience	Positivity	Power
17	Q	Quality	Quintessence	Quiet
18	R	Reliance	Rejuvenation	Resolve
19	S	Stillness	Strength	Splendor
20	T	Truth	Temperance	Trust
21	U	Universal	Ultimate	Unity
22	V	Vibrancy	Venerable	Valor
23	W	Worth	Wonder	Weave
24	X	Xenodochial	Xenial	X
25	Y	Yin/Yang	Yen	Yield
26	Z	Zenith	Zeal	Zappy
27	all enduring abuse	Fearlessness	Healing	
28	all suffering depression	Balance	Hope	
29	all caught in addiction	Recovery	Sobriety	
30	all preparing for death	Openness	Light	

Dedicate the Merit

This is the traditional Buddhist prayer
    centering one's intention on the good of the world.
"Merit" is all the good you create from your actions.
You dedicate or commit all your good karma to all creation.

"By this merit, may all obtain omniscience.
May it defeat the enemy, wrongdoing.

From the stormy waves of birth, old age, sickness and death,
>from the ocean of samsara, may I free all beings."[38]

Read for Authenticity
Read how you walk in your authenticity.
>Experience your own authenticity.
>Savor your own unique self.

Read for blocks to your authenticity.
>In what situations do you become less authentic?

What expectations of family hinder your authenticity?
Expectations of church?   Of your job?   Of society?

Integrating Bead Meditation
This meditation integrates the prayers of six different religions.
The prayers or chants are repeated and counted out]
>on prayer beads.

I choose to use the Muslim beads:
>where there are ninety-nine beads on the string
>symbolizing the ninety-nine names of God in the Qur'an.

The beads are usually divided into groups of thirty-three beads.

For each bead in the section of thirty-three,
>repeat the prayer or chant from that religious tradition.

I have provided several options.

OPTION A:	NAME OF THE DIVINE	
Indigenous	Kitche Manitou	
	"Great Spirit" in Ojibwe	
	Wakan Tanka	
	"Great Mystery" in Dakota	
Buddhism	O Enlightened One	
Islam	The Wise or The Guide	
	Two of 99 names of God In Qu'ran	
Christianity	Creator, Savior, Spirit	
Judaism	Adonai" or El Shaddai	
	"Lord"" or "God Almighty"	
Hinduism	OM	
	"That Thou Art"	
	Considered sound of "God."	
OPTION B:	CHANT OF PRAISE	
Indigenous	May I always walk in beauty.	
	Ancient Native Indian Prayer	
Buddhism	Om mani padme hum.	
	"Behold! The jewel of lotus"	
	Oldest Buddhist chant	
	believed to contain all the teachings of Buddha.	
Islam	La Ilaha Illallah.	
	"There is no God but Allah."	
	"Allah" is "God" in Arabic.	

---

[38] Traditional Buddhist prayer recited before meditation.

Christianity	Glory be to the Father, to the Son, to the Holy Spirit	
	The first line from the prayer "Glory Be".	

Christianity   Glory be to the Father, to the Son, to the Holy Spirit
        The first line from the prayer "Glory Be".

Judaism   Barukh atah Adonai,
       Eloheinu, melekh ha'olam
         "Blessed are you, Lord, God,
         sovereign of the universe"

Hinduism   Har or Hara
        "Creative Infinity"

OPTION C: **PRAYER OF INTENTION**
Ingenious   For the good of all with harm toward none.
        Last line of Pagan blessing

Buddhism   Enlightenment is achieved
      by practicing wisdom and compassion.
        Mantra of Avalokiteshvara,
        Bodhisattva of Compassion

Islam   Allahu akbar.
        "God is Great."

Christianity   Not my will, but Yours be done.
        Luke 22: 42

Judaism   May I act justly, love tenderly, and walk humble with God.
        Micah 6:8

Hinduism   Sat Nam.
        "Truth is my identity"'

OPTION D: **PRAYER**
Ingenious   May I learn the lessons You have hidden in creation.
        Chief Yellow Lark

Buddhism   Because I am alive, all things are possible.
        Mantra of Thich Nhat Hanh[39]

Islam   Bismilah. Er-Rahman, Er-Rahim
        "We begin in name of Allah,
        Most Merciful, Most Compassionate."
        First line from first Surrah or chapter, in Qur'an

Christianity   Make me an instrument of your peace.
        Prayer of Francis of Assisi.

Judaism   The heavens declare of the glory of God.
        Psalm 19: 2

Hinduism   Lead me from falsehood to truth,
       from despair to hope; from fear to trust.
        The Paramahamsa rom The Upanishad

---

[39] Thích Nhât Hành Quotes, http://www.goodreads.com/author/quotes/9074.Th_ch_Nh_t_H_nh (December 12, 2014).

OPTION E:	INTENT OF EACH TRADITION
Ingenious	May I be one with all creation.
Buddhism	May I be conscious.
Islam	May I surrender to God's will.
Christianity	May I love my enemies.
Judaism	May I heal the world.
Hinduism	May I relentlessly pursue truth.

Read for Shortcomings
Read for your shortcomings.
Make a searching and fearless moral inventory of yourself
Go deep into your personality, intentions, and behaviors.

Then admit to yourself, to God
    and to another human being [trusted mentor]
    the exact nature of your shortcomings
    and wrongs committed.[40]

Compassionate Abiding Practice[41]
This practice was created by Buddhist Pema Chodron
    to aid people in dealing with reactive emotions.

It is a method of releasing the emotion
    that is causing pain or blockage.
Do this practice on the spot
    in the moment a reactive emotion is acknowledged.

When something irritates you
    impatience, frustration, anger, boredom, panic, etc.
    breathe in that emotion
    breathe out space for that emotion.
For example, breathe in ""impatience";
    breathe out space for "impatience".

Next, drop the story line
    the internal dialogue that might arise with your impatience
    and focus on the emotion.
The story line fuels emotion and therefore fuels your suffering.
If you entertain any story line about impatience
    you will just increase you impatience.

Mantras on the Gifts of the 2nd Chakra
A. Breathe in "fearlessness"; breathe out "courage".
B. Breathe in "enlightenment"; breathe out "awareness".
C. Breathe in "consciousness"; breathe out "consciousness".

---

[40] Alcoholics Anonymous, 59.
[41] Pema Chodron, Session One 1.8, "Awakening Love", Jan 13 - Mar 6, 2011, audio tape, Sound Tunes, Gampo Abbey, Cape Breton, Nova Scotia, 2012.

2nd GIFTS

1. When I am fully present   I am consciousness.

2. When I am real, honest,
    and genuine   I am authenticity.

3. When I own and healthily
    express my emotions   I am alive.

4. When I appreciate all my talents   I am creativity.

5. When I face my fears   I am fearlessness.

6. When I release the past as a lesson,
    do the work of today,
    and allow the future to unfold
    as should without anxiety   I am present.

7. When my second chakra is open
    with good boundaries   I am.

3. BALANCING POWER

PHILOSOPHY OF POWER

Power is the energy that generates wholeness.
It is the force all of creation uses to develop and enhance life.

In the chakra system, each chakra builds on the ones below it.
The third chakra's concept of power
    is one of combination and interaction.[42]
Its gift is in its solidarity and integration with other energies:
    human, animal, material, spiritual, divine.

Power is the force that is our individual autonomy
    allowing us to "be "free and interdependent
    in all areas of being
    [physically, emotionally, mentally, and spiritually]. [43]
When we stand in our power, we know the sense of "being" whole.
Everything in creation has power.

As power is the energy force to 'be";
    will is our ability to utilize that power
    in time and space for action.
The will is what makes things happen.

When we are whole, we assert our will in all manners healthy for us.
We stand in our power and use it to heal ourselves and the world.
But often, our will is compromised in some form
    and we misuse our power.
The following graphic, called the "power wheel", illustrates
    how we move through different stages of power.

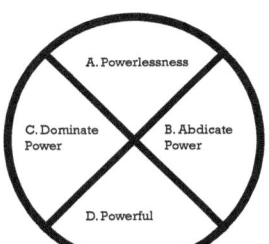

A. Powerlessness
Powerlessness is the state of having no power to affect a situation.
In this state, being in control or utilizing our will is absent.
We, consciously or unconsciously,
    do not possess the ability to act for ourselves.
Many forms of powerlessness are navigated during childhood.
As an infant, someone must feed me, carry me, change me.
    I am totally dependent and powerless.
As we mature, we learn how to use power to take care of ourselves
    and be interdependent.
Once we are chronologically adults, we are in charge of our lives.
This is our domain of individuality
    we are responsible for our movements, actions, behaviors,
    thoughts, emotions, relationships, communication, vision.

The third chakra's great lesson is that indeed we have power
    and can utilize our will to be authentically alive persons.
I have the power to create who I am and who I wish to be.

But the lesson does not stop there
    because there are many things I do not control.
I am not all powerful nor do I control the universe.

As a human being [as well as an addict], my task is to comprehend
    where I am powerful and where I am powerless.

---

[42] Judith, 179.
[43] Judith, 179.

This is the heart of the serenity prayer:
    "God grant me
    the serenity to accept the things I cannot change,
    the courage to change the things I can,
    and the wisdom to know the difference."[44]

This prayer starts by stating the reality that we need to admit
    that some things are beyond our control.
Sometimes our task is accepting our powerlessness—
    recognizing and admiring that many things
    are beyond our control.

I do not have power over other people:
    not over their emotions, attitudes, or behaviors.
I do not have power over most situations in my life:
    stop lights, the weather, Wall Street, my boss's mood,
    my partner's happiness, the Pope, or the neighbor's cat.

As a recovery drug addict,
    I am powerless over my many addictions.
The world is unfolding as it should
    d and I am not the one in charge of any of it.

Our difficulty is sometimes we get stuck in powerlessness
    in places where we indeed are meant to be powerful
    and times when we are stuck in thinking we are powerful
    in places where we indeed are powerless.
Being conscious of emotions and intentions
    brings me to the truth of my power.
For example, if I am unconscious of my anger at a friend
    I can easily become passive aggressive
    demonstrating my power inappropriately.
When I am aware and conscious of my anger, deal with my emotions
    then I will lead with my power and not abuse that power.

While I am powerless to change others and many situations in life,
    I am fully responsible for me
    and fully responsible to change the things I can.

I heard a variation of the Serenity Prayer I also appreciate as truth:
    "God, grant me
    the serenity to accept the people I cannot change,
    the courage to change the one I can,
    and the wisdom to know it's me."

Growing up in a very abusive environment
    there was a lot of programing by my parents and others.
My beliefs were dictated; my actions controlled.
As an adult, I felt powerless in many situations
    to think or act for myself.
I could not break free from dictates of my dysfunctional past.
Not utilizing my will, I felt paralyzed.

It took me years to understand that I was the only one
    who could change my thoughts and actions
    to regain my own power.

---

[44] Twelve Steps and Twelve Traditions, (New York City, NY: AA Worldwide Services), 41.

Wisdom is the gift of understanding reality—
> what do I need to accept, what do I need to change.

It is a necessity in knowing my areas of powerlessness
> and powerfulness.

B. Abdicate Power

The next stage of the power wheel is "Abdicating Power".
Its relationship to Dominating Power is not coincidental;
> they are the opposite sides of the same coin.

Both are motivated by fear; both are the antithesis of wholeness.
Neither embraces healthy solidarity—
> integration with other energies.

Abdicating power means we have, consciously or unconsciously
> given away our power.

Believing our energy isn't constructive or strong enough
> we utilize our will to surrender some of our power.

This misuse of energy is not life-giving
> and it happens in multiple, common situations.

We may relinquish our power by using
> people, attitudes, and objects to feel important.

False idols include symbols of status we mistake for true power:
>> having the "right" clothes, or car or toys or address
>> seeking the prestigious title just for the title.

False power by association is another type of idolatry:
>> knowing or associating with the "right" people,
>> procuring a "trophy wife or husband",
>> being a name-dropper to impress others.

A more serious type of abdicating our power
> is abdicating out of fear
> to allow another person to control us.

Our will is squelched and we acquiesce to the other's demands,
> whether those demands are reasonable or not.

Perhaps we fear we are not powerful enough
> or perhaps we fear our own powerfulness.

Either way, we relinquish our power to someone
> it does not belong to.

This is not the same as negotiating with another.
In relationships there needs to be a mutual give and take—
> sometimes I give and sometimes my partner gives.

That is healthy.
Unhealthy is when I do all the giving.

Some will stay in the abdicating power stage all of their lifetime.
If we succeed in moving past it
> most of us move to misusing power by dominating others.

This is the cycle of abuse: the victim becomes the perpetrator.
Having been controlled by another
> we seek to be in the position of control over others.

C. Dominate Power

Dominating power is taking power,
> unconsciously or consciously, that is not ours.

Because we fear being powerless
>> we utilize our will to dominate in order to feel in control.
This misuse of energy is not life-giving
>> and it also happens in multiple, common situations.
We may demonstrate our domination by:
>> withholding or showering people
>>>> with money, toys, or affection
>> having to always be "right", always better than others,
>> acting cocky, superior, self-righteous.

We are the bully: aggressive, domineering, hostile, violent.
Remember violence extends beyond just the physical.
It includes insults, threats, intimidation, and coercion.

Winning is most important in this stage of power.
It includes acquiring the most money, biggest office, most control.
>> And we seek to win at all costs.
If that is our goal, compromise and negotiation
>> are not part of the plan.
We believe we are better, more important,
>> and have the right answers.
Others should just obey.
Wounding others is not our concern; being the most important is.

Most of us are in either the abdicating or dominating stage.
A few of us might even gravitate to one in our personal life
>> and the other in our professional life.

The third chakra tends to be unhealthy in American society
>> because we are taught to misuse power and will.
We are trained to listen to the ego, focus on material attainment,
>> collect "stuff" as the signal of success,
>> to be motivated by the "more is better" mentality.
We stay in our heads and we stay empty.

Concentrating on the cognitive
>> we ignore and silence the heart and the soul.
We also ignore and silence the gift
>> of the abundant diversity of creativity.
So our expression of creativity gets shut down or stifled.
Conformity, inertia, and stagnation set in
>> as we abdicate or dominate power.

When we get stuck in abdicating or dominating power
>> the energies can grow beyond the individual person
>> to affect the greater world.

As a single individual, I am in one of the stages of the power wheel.
But groups and organizations
>> [families, clubs, athletic organizations, churches,
>> schools, businesses, governments]
>>>> also fit into the circle of power.

All of us will be involved with some organizations that misuse power
>> and it is vital to recognize when one is caught up in
>> the machinery of a dysfunctional system.[45]

[45] Bergeson.

"Machinery systems" are places where power is abused
        to squelch and de-humanize individuals
        within that system.
The following signal that you are in a machine system:
        any place where you are treated like a nonentity;
        you lose energy and get drained;
        you feel like you're a cog in the machine;
        you feel mentality that someone or something owns you;
        rather than being empowered,
        you feel stripped of power.

If we are conscious of our self-talk
        we will hear revealing statements
        that something needs to shift.
When you are disengaged, you say, "I quit" on some level.
You may not turn in your keys to the boss but at the very minimum
        your energy stops engaging with the person or situation.
When you are dissatisfied, you may say, "I used to be someone,
        but now I feel unimportant or undervalued here."
When you are disorientated, you may say, "Where do I fit in?"
When you are disenchanted,
        you say, "This is awful, terrible, horrible!"
No longer optimistic,
        you dwell on the negative hopelessness of the job.
With all these positions, change needs to occur.

In many ways, the machine system is like the feudal system.
Feudal systems had lords who held all the power, money, affluence
        and the serfs who did the work without fair compensation
        or recognition or any real power in the organization.

Is this not like the scenario of many American companies?
The CEO gets millions of dollars
        and the workers get minimum wage.

Because American society struggles with power
        many of our businesses and churches operating in a machine mentality
        struggling with issues of justice and equity.

Buying into the machinery system is an option but not a healthy one.
When we are used by systems, we end up being spent and empty.
If you identify that you are in one, you have two healthy options:
        1] work on contributing to change the system;
        2] disengage yourself, pull away, or leave the system.

The more people involved, the greater the energy.
As said earlier, what we focus on will grow.
One can choose to use one's power or join a movement
        to heal the world or hurt the world.
Gandhi and Hitler, living at the same time
        both used power to further their respective causes.
But being in very different places on the power wheel,
        their outcomes and legacies were very different.

D. Powerful

Being in your power is the stage of authentic adulthood.
It is our ability to "be" who we are—
> grounded, centered, authentic, whole.

Abusing power by abdication or domination will eventually
> leave us wanting
>> because neither of these stages is authentic.

True power is an internal, not an external, force.
It can never come from outside myself,
> can never come from another person or material item.
Power always comes from within me.

The challenge of the third chakra is to learn to do life differently:
to learn to listen to one's self, to learn
to stand in one's power with integrity.
When we walk in authentic power, we live in humility.
These two attributes are twins.

Power is not arrogance
> but an honest accounting of who we are at our core.
Humility is not cowardice
> but the same honest accounting of who we are at our core.

Standing in my power, I want to be "marshmallow titanium"
> gentle on the outside, steel on the inside.
When people confront me, I want to respond like a marshmallow:
> not harsh, abrasive, rude, or reactionary
> but lenient, calm, compassionate, tolerant.
This does not mean giving in; it means
> not reacting defensively or dominantly.

On the inside, at my core, I desire to be like titanium
> possessing unbreakable self-worth,
>> unwavering integrity, and an indomitable spirit.

Power and the will to utilize our power are our birthright.
Standing in our power, we act in the world with integrity.
When we stand in our power
> we can encourage others to stand in theirs.
Standing in authentic power, we know power from within—
> from the integration of body and soul
> from our connections to earth and Divinity.

The Entity Called "God"

Powerlessness is an incredible teacher about God.
When I truly cannot manage my life or effect change
> there is an answer to my powerlessness—
> that answer is "God".

Whatever name you use,
> [Higher Power, the Divine, the Universe, Truth, Light,
> Jesus, Creator, Consciousness, Allah, Yahweh,
> Love, Diana, Grace, Brahman, God]
> there is Something greater than humanity,
> Something that or Someone who empowers us to fullness.

Remember all our words for the Divine are metaphors—
        descriptions of what we believe God is.
But because metaphors and analogies limit as well as define,
        the words we think clarify who or what God is
        actually restrict our understanding of who or what God is.
        If God is "Father", then God can't be "Mother".
        If God is "Creator", then God can't be "Destroyer".

Yet the paradox of the Divine is that God is both
        Father and Mother, Creator and Destroyer.
The irony of God is that God is
        both the Incomprehensible Mystery
        and Personally Known.

Humans tend to focus on the latter
        because we cannot identify the former.
If God to me is loving, merciful, and healing,
        I can understand those qualities—
        they are human qualities also.
But how can I name or describe or have a relationship with
        an Incomprehensible Mystery?

Because the Divine is beyond our definition
        it is vital to use a variety of names for the Divine
        to help us discover the breadth
        and depth of this entity called God.
Begin with what the masters taught.
World religions have paved the way to greater understanding
        of who the Divine is, how God works in the world,
        and paths to building a relationship
        with our Higher Power.

We are part of this entity called God,
        not the totality of the Divine
        but part of this Supreme Power.
As a human being in a physical body
        our task is to realize that connection.
We seek this relationship and we are unsatisfied
        unfulfilled until we develop a partnership with the Divine.

Examine the following chart.
Learn what the ancients have taught.
Listen, study, ponder, search, wrestle.
If one or more organized spiritual paths resonate with you, follow it.
If not, create your own.

TRADITION	NAME OF "GOD"	SACRED TEXTS	"GOD" IN THE WORLD
AMERICAN INDIAN	Kitche Manitou "Great Spirit" [Ojibwe] Wakan Tanka "Great Mystery" [Dakota]	Predominately an oral way of life, not written down	Great Spirit is alive in all creation. Mother Earth gives life to the body; Great Spirit gives life to the soul.
BUDDHISM	Non-theistic Some say Buddha is God Consciousness	Dhammapada The Upanishads	Officially, no belief In "God" but belief is not prohibited.
ISLAM	Allah "God"	Qur'an	God created humankind.
CHRISTIANITY	God Jesus Holy Spirit	Bible	God created humankind. Jesus is God-among-us.
JUDIASM	Yahweh "God" Elhoim "God" Adonai "Lord"	Tanahk	God created humankind. Has covenant with us.
HINDUISM	The Source Brahman "Unchanging Reality"	The Upanishads Bhadavad Gita The Vedas	Every part of creation is Divine. Nothing exist apart from God.

Spirituality teaches a universal truth regarding power's true nature:
    it is indeed an energy of collaboration, not separation.
We are invited to a relationship of collegiality and partnership
    with each other, with all creation, and with the Divine.

All relationships require the same ingredients:
    truthful communication of speaking and listening,
    trust earned on both sides,
    the relationship's importance and priority demonstrated
        by frequent and honest interaction,
    openness and willingness to learn
        the depths of each other,

        love and respect as the foundations of the partnership.
The relationship with the Divine requires the same effort.

This Divine-human partnership means we will be asked
        to learn and grow.
After all, that is why we are on this planet—
        to learn how to be a fully alive human person.
When God asks us to do something we find easy to do,
        saying "yes" is also easy.
Even if God asks us to do something difficult,
        when we have to surrender our will
            and know this path is best,
        courage, strength, and commitment carry us
            to do as asked.
When God asks us to do something difficult
        that we do not want to do,
        our answer might be "no" to the Divine.
This is part of our humanity—the inner battle.
I call this the civil war of the person.
 Part of me knows I need to do what is asked
        and another part of me just can't agree to do it.
When this happens, consider carefully your motives and fear.
If you can overcome the fear, perhaps "yes" will be your answer.
If you cannot overcome the fear, qualify your "no".
You can say "no but" meaning "No, I can't do this but I can do that."
You can say, "No, I can't do this today
        but I will work on being able to do it tomorrow."
As a partner with the Divine, you can negotiate.

I always felt there was a Higher Power
        but have not always worked to build a relationship.
One single aspect of the partnership scared me greatly:
        surrendering to the Divine.
All religions teach that fundamental concept using different words:
        surrender, doing the will of God, submitting to God,
        conforming with Divine will,
        turning one's will and life over to God.

I knew that surrender was the heart of this partnership
        with the Divine but I struggled with it.
Yes, I wanted help but I also wanted to be in control.
Yes, I would do what God asked as long as I could do it my way.

But this partnerships doesn't work that way.
And in the wisdom of Big Book of AA,
        "the result was nil until we let go absolutely."[46]
What I discovered was that I feared the eradication of self.
In reality what transpires in a partnership with the Divine
        is a fulfillment of self.
Within this partnership, I discover who I am and why I am here.

---

[46] Alcoholics Anonymous, 58.

3rd FUNDAMENTALS

3rd Chakra Basics

Location	From the top of the pelvis to the bottom of the ribs Solar plexus
Color	Yellow
Relation	Islam
Governs	1. Power
	2. Will
	3. Habits
	4. Interaction with the world

1. Power

Power is the energy that generates wholeness.
As the force of our individual autonomy,
    power promotes freedom and interdependence
        in all areas of being.
When we stand in our power, we know the sense of "being" whole.

2. Will

Power is the energy force to "be";
    will is our ability to utilize that power
        in time and space for action.
The task of the will is to overcome inertia.[47]

When we are whole, we assert our will in all manners healthy for us.
We stand in our power and use it to heal ourselves and the world.
But often, our will is compromised in some form
        and we misuse our power.
The following indicate difficulty within the third chakra.[48]
Powerless statements are:

There's no solution.	I can't do this.
It's hopeless.	Why do I have to do this?
I'm lost.	Take care of me.

Abdicate power statements are:	Dominating statements are:
You have the right answer.	Mine is the only solution.
I don't know what to do.	It's my way.
I always want help.	I don't need help.
Anyone could do it better than me.	Only I can do this.

Once we identify what stage we are in,
    we can create options for change.
Patterns, attitudes, and habits can all be changed
        with intention and practice.
Then we can assert our will in accordance with our highest good.

3. Habits

The third chakra is where we develop our habits.
This includes all patterns we have to get what we want or need

---

[47] Judith, 185.
[48] Bergeson.

as well as all patterns we have to get
what we don't want or need.
Weaving Islam to the third chakra is a testament
to the Muslim dedication to prayer.
Muslims stop to connect to the Divine wherever they are,
whatever they are doing, five times throughout the day.

This is a committed, faith-filled, and ambitious practice
that all people would benefit from.
This dedication to prayer invites us to examine
our own prayer schedules in particular
and our habits in general.

The task of conscious living is to investigate our habits and patterns,
to advance the ones that are healthy for us and
to eliminate the ones that no longer serve
our greater good.
Remember energy abhors a vacuum.
If you try to break a habit or pattern
you need to replace it with something else.

Habits take thirty repetitions to learn and maintain.
They demand attention and positive reinforcement
combined with courage and strength
to overcome resistance.
Call it resistance or temptation or wrestling with demons,
the struggle to change attitudes
and behavior can be difficult.
Any honest human has stories of failed attempts, derailments,
and relapses.

Do not be discouraged.
Change is hard work, worth the effort
and will happen given energy.
Work actively with resistance—fighting it will only engage it further.
The more I "fought" with my overeating
by being angry at myself an belittling my efforts,
the more I ate and the worse the temptation.
Only when I accepted my own struggles
and acknowledged the temptations,
could I learn new eating habits.

Listen to your body, heart, and mind.
What messages are you sending and receiving?
What do you feel?
What old tapes are you hearing?
What is your fear?
Where in your body are you holding tension?

As you listen to yourself
you will understand your resistance and how to disarm it.
Change is an absolute necessity in life—all life does is change!
Adulthood is learning to embrace the changes courageously.

4. Interaction With The World
The third chakra governs how one walks in the world.
This includes how we present ourselves

    anywhere in the public sector:
    at our jobs, gym, restaurants, businesses, traveling.
The emotions we feel are rooted in the second chakra
    and then get expressed to the greater world in the third.
    Am I meek? Confident? Exhausted? Demanding?
Whatever I feel, it is manifested in my outward behavior and energy
    as I engage in the world throughout my day.

Road rage is a good example.
If I am angry at a partner and deny the anger or don't express it,
    the first driver who I perceive as driving inappropriately,
    will get my horn and a dose of my misplaced anger.
The emotions from my family situation have spilled over
    to my greater world.

This is a microcosmic example of most of the world's problems:
    we walk in the world, expressing our emotions
    to the wrong person, in the wrong way, at the wrong time.

Consequently we have road rage, street violence, and global war.
Walking in the world authentically means we use our power and will
    to deal with emotion in an appropriately healthy fashion.
This is the only way to effect real change to heal ourselves
    and the world.

Putting plans in time and space is also part of the third chakra.
When I create something in the second
    it stays in formation until I put it into action.
Writing this book is a good example.
I thought about writing, generated ideas for years.
 Even tried writing but quit after an extensively laborious few pages.
I could create the concepts in my second chakra
    but until it was time to be put out into the world on paper,
    the creation stayed in my second chakra.
This is not a bad thing.
Life is about timing
    and trusting the timing that is not always in one's control.

The most valuable lesson to learn is to do the work
    and then let go of the outcome.
The AA phrase "doing the next right thing" is the first step[49]
    What do I need to do today?
    What is my responsibility today?

Buddhists teach well the second part of the lesson—
    let go of the outcome.
This is very difficult yet essential.
Using power well does not mean I will always get my way.
When I let go of the outcome, I accept my place in the world.
I seek to avoid both
    the egotism of thinking I am in control
        if the outcome is to my liking
    or the depression of thinking I am a failure
        if the outcome is not.
The adult's job is to stand in power,
    take the action that needs to be taken
    and surrender the outcome to my Higher Power.

---

[49] AA Motto.

Glass Body

Energetically putting on a "glass body" guards you
        from energies you do not want in your space.
The concept is to run a protective energy around yourself,
        from the feet to the crown of the head,
        from the skin outwards in all directions 6-20 inches.
You can envision this protective energy as flexible glass, Plexiglas,
        or any other transparent, impenetrable, limber substance.
Some situations are more charged for us.
Perhaps you are meeting with someone angry, resentful, mean;
        or someone who is needy and clingy,
        or bossy and difficult.
Any time you have difficulty maintaining healthy boundaries
        put on a glass body.
The energy you encounter will hit the glass body, not you.
Because the protection is transparent
        you can see the energy in order to evaluate it.
Perhaps it is energy you do not want or need.
        You can let it slide down the glass body, into the earth.
Perhaps it is energy you do want or need and is healthy for you.
        You can take in its truth and use it as you need it.
If the energy sticks to the glass body
        it is a message that this energy is an issue for you.
Pay attention to what is this energy trying to teach you?
        What do you need to do? Or not do?

The point is, with a glass body, the energy will not overtake you.
It will help identify your issues and areas of learning.
You can maintain good boundaries
        and then be able to make clear decisions for yourself.

If the situation is extremely dangerous for you,
        envision something stronger than glass
        for your protective energy.
I have used armor, chain-mail, and even three layers of Plexiglas
        on occasion.
But I wear it rarely and only as long as I need to
        for it is too heavy and energy consuming to wear often.

When the third chakra is balanced
        we can stand and act in our authentic power.
We are aware of all the patterns we use to get
        what we want and need
        as well as all the patterns we use to get
        what we don't want or need.

3rd Synopsis

When the third chakra is compromised,
        I do not use power effectively.
I seek to either control others or let others control me.

When the third chakra is healthy, I understand and accept
        the areas of my life where I am powerless.
I stand in my power, grounded and conscious of who I am,
        willing to develop habits that promote my highest good.
I can walk in the world authentically and powerfully me.

3rd PRACTICES

Read 3rd Chakra
Read for strengths in the third chakra.
Read your solar plexus.   What do you see? Hear? Feel? Know?
Read your abdomen   What do you see? Hear? Feel? Know?
What are the strengths of your third chakra?
Celebrate the strengths and power of your third chakra.

Read the blocks in the third chakra.
Read your solar plexus.   Gleam lessons from your blocks.
Read your abdomen.   Gleam lessons from your blocks.
Do you perceive any patterns?   Gleam lessons from them.

Glass Body
Ground.
Say "No / Goodbye" to all energies not your own
Ask all energies not yours to move six feet away from you.
Imagine pouring water over your head that completely covers you
        touching every square centimeter of your skin.
Envision the water hardening to glass, then to flexible Plexiglas.

A glass body will keep energy that is not yours
        from having as much impact when it hits.
Most will slide off.
What does not slide off, sticks to highlight your issues.
What are your red flags?
What are their lessons?

Shortcomings Revisited
Following up from the second chakra practice
        of admitting shortcomings,
        now is the time to be entirely ready
        to have God remove them all.
This may alert you to your desire to hold on to your shortcomings.[50]
Analyze your motives and fears.
Recognize where you are powerless and powerful.
Allow willingness to lead;
        then humbly ask God to remove all your shortcomings.[51]

The Entity Called God: Childhood and Adulthood
Define the God of your childhood
How did you interact with God?
What did God do all day?
What was God's role?
What was yours?

Define the God of your adulthood.
How are those views similar?
How are they different?
Who do you want or need God to be today?
What old concepts need releasing?
What new descriptors do you need to embrace?

---
[50] Alcoholics Anonymous, 59.
[51] Alcoholics Anonymous, 59.

What are your fears of having a new concept of the Divine?
How does God communicate with You today?
How would you like God to communicate with you?

Read for Power
Read for your use of power.
Where are you powerless?
> What are your fears?

Where are you abdicating power?
> What are your fears?

Where are you dominating power?
> What are your fears?

Where are you powerful?
> What are your fears?

Read for your level of acceptance of things you cannot control.
Read for your level of courage to change the things you can control.
Read for your level of wisdom in knowing the difference.

Naming the Divine
Define "God".
Who or what do you think "God" is?
Write down the words you frequently use for the Divine.
Analyze your list.
> Do you have adjectives, verbs, or nouns?
> Do you use male, female, or non-gender language?

What types of behavior do you expect from God
> based on your language?

For example if you pray to God as Father '
> are you looking for protection?

Write down an antonym for each word.
Use the antonyms for a few weeks to broaden your definition of God.

Space and Time with the Divine
Create a prayer space.
Make a prayer space so you can go to the same place
> every prayer time.

Seek a place of solitary quiet.
What articles do you want or need in your space?
> Candles, incense, sage, pictures, statues, beads?
> Chair, pillow, meditation cushion?

Read for Machinery Systems
Read for the machinery systems in your life.
How do you choose to handle them?
Where can you find healing and rejuvenating energy?

Create a prayer schedule
Consider creating a prayer schedule with specific times
> throughout the day
> > that you will spend time with the Divine.

Most religions encourage daily prayer.
Consider the rigor of Islam.
Muslims pray five times each day in order to reconnect to God often.
How often would you like to pray?
How often do you need to pray?
Remember prayer does not need to be long—
    it can be as simple as bringing your consciousness to God
    or resetting an intention
    or it could be a verbal prayer of one word.

The point is to improve your contact and relationship with the Divine
    by remembering God throughout the day.
Seek to increase the number of times you pray by one.

Read for Habits
Read your habits.
Which habits have you built that are healthy for you?
Celebrate them.
Which habits are unhealthy or harmful for you today?
Are you ready and willing to change them?
    If not, gently consider why not.
    If so, consider what steps you need to build a new habit.

Steps to Building New Habits
1] Read for what the new path or behavior you want or need?
    [This is soul work.]

2] Think about what needs to change.
What will be the hurdles or barriers to change?
How will you handle those challenges?
What will help reinforce the new habit?
    [This is mind work.]

3] Consider your emotional shifts
When you let go of an old habit and start a new one.
Carve out time to listen to your emotions and give them a voice.
Plan some ways to deal with the fear or anxiety that may occur.
    [This is heart work.]

4] Decide on the first step of action.
Take small steps to reduce chances of failure and maximize success.
Be gentle.
    [This is body work.]
Most of us have repeated this pattern dozens or hundreds of times
    in our efforts to overcome one habit.
You did not get your old habits overnight,
    you will not change them overnight.
Progress is the goal, not perfection.

Prayer and God
Play with postures and movements.
Prayer can be verbal or physical or spiritual.
Most of us get the verbal but movement and gestures in prayer
    are more challenging.
Experiment freely with various body positions.

Raise the arms or the palms.
Stand, kneel, bow, or prostrate one's body.
Dance, chant, drum, sing.

Generate a variety of prayer types:
adoration which praises the Divine
gratitude which expresses thanksgiving
petition which asks for Divine help
repentance which asks for forgiveness
meditation which seeks to be in Divine presence
contemplation which is active listening to the Divine
bliss which is union with the Divine.

Consider what types of prayer you use most frequently.
Analyze your choices.
Why are these favorites?
How can you add variety to your prayer?

Challenges with the Entity Called God
There are many hurdles of building a quality relationship with God.
Are you too busy?
It's setting priorities:
forgo something to choose something more valuable.

Are you afraid?
Of course, we all are!
This is uncharted territory into unknown depths of Mystery.
And you are not in control.
Admit it, claim it, own it, feel it, accept it—then pray anyway.

Are you unsure what to do?
The answer is to listen.
Shut up, be still, and listen.
How are you answering the Divine?
Consider carefully your motives.
Why are you saying "yes", if "yes" is your answer?
If you are saying "no", why are you resisting?

What is your fear?
Can you say "no, but...."?

Have you been asked to do the same thing multiple times?
What is the significance of this?

Mantras on the Gifts of the 3rd Chakra
A. Breathe in "humility"; breathe out "power".
B. Breathe in "determination"; breathe out "strength".
C. Breathe in "dignity"; breathe out "dignity".

3rd GIFTS

1. When I stand in
        my authenticity   I am power.

2. When I partner
        with the Divine   I am prayer.

3. When I accept the things
        I cannot change,
        change the things I can,
        and recognize the difference`   I am integrity.

4. When I authentically walk
        in the world   I am strength.

5. When I stand in my power
        without abdication
        or domination   I am courage.

6. When I say "yes" to the Divine   I am God's will.

7. When my third chakra is open
        with good boundaries   I am.

4. RUTHLESS COMPASSION

PHILOSOPHY OF COMPASSION

Compassion is love.
What a simple, multi-defined, overworked,
                all-encompassing concept.
At its heart, love is seeking the highest good
        for one's self and another.
Love is the intention, attitude, and behavior
        of seeking the best for someone,
        even if the best is not what one wants.

Love's essence is union; its mission is connection;
        its method is acceptance; its goal is healing.

Love's Essence is Union

Compassion is the foundation of all great spiritual traditions.
Whether eloquently defining love or artistically challenging us to love,
        we learn much from the Masters throughout history.

The Islamic Qur'an identifies the qualities of compassion.
Love is true sacrifice." 2:177   "Love is steadfast." 3:146
Love is reliance on God." 3:159   "Love is natural." 14:3
Love is not obsessive." 4:107   "Love is intimate." 7:1
Love does not decay." 49:12   "God is Love." 11:91

For Christians, Paul's stunning language of love
        is 1st Corinthians 13.
"Love is patient, love is kind.
It does not envy, it does not boast, it is not proud.
It does not dishonor others, it is not self-seeking,
It is not easily angered, it keeps no record of wrongs.
Love does not delight in evil but rejoices with the truth.
It always protects, always trusts always hopes, always perseveres.
Love never fails....
And now these three remain: faith, hope and love.
But the greatest of these is love.'

Buddhism often uses the phrase "Loving-kindness"
        to depict the four qualities of Love:
        openness, joy, appreciation, and equanimity.
The spirit of the Buddha is that of great loving kindness
        and compassion to help all people.

This great compassion is the spirit that prompts us to be ill
        with the illness of all people to suffer with their suffering.[52]

Considered by most to be the greatest Jewish prayer,
        the Shema in Deut. 6
        proclaims the totality of our love for the Divine.
"Hear, O Israel!
The Lord is our God; the Lord is One.
And you shall love the Lord, your God,
        with all your heart
        and with all your soul,
        and with all your being.
These words, which I command you, shall be upon your heart."

---

[52] The Society for the Promotion of Buddhism, The Teachings of Buddha, (Tokyo, Japan: Kosaido Printing Company, 1966), 28.

The highest of all Ojibwe life principles is "Namaji":
    respect, dignity, honor, and pride.[53]
As one walks the Good Red Road, [this life's path],
    we walk in Namaji, in harmony with all creation,
    doing good for the community.
In most Native Indian cultures, the well-being of the group
    is more important than that of a particular person.
Helping others is the priority because the welfare of the community
    surpasses the welfare of the individual.

The Bhargava Gita, one of the sacred texts of Hinduism,
    clearly declares the Divine's purpose for love in 10:11.
"Out of compassion for them, I, dwelling in their hearts,
    destroy with the shining lamp of knowledge
    the darkness born of ignorance."

Indeed, the absence of love is ignorance.
That ignorance conceals itself as hatred, jealousy, greed, prejudice.
Whereas these aspects are more easily identified,
    ignorance is more subtle and is harder to admit.
No one wants to be thought of as dumb.
But stupidity is not the definition of ignorance.
Ignorance means to be oblivious or unaware.
So the real question is: what are we ignoring?

When we find ourselves lacking love, we are ignoring love's union.
All creation is united as part of the Divine.
The parts I see in you that I don't like are actually
    the parts in me I don't like.
If I can reject you, perhaps I can deny the parts that you and I share.
    And I choose separation rather than union.

Love's Mission Is Connection
When I refuse to love,
    I am ignoring and refusing to be connected to you.
Perhaps I believe I will not get hurt if I build my walls—
    walls so distant or dense
    that you cannot get through them—
    but in keeping you out, I imprison myself.
Walls bring isolation, not connection.

Love's Method Is Acceptance
. Love is acceptance with no exceptions.
While some of us have wounds that are more readily apparent;
    some of us have masked our wounds remarkably well.
When I reject love, I ignore your wounds.
    Maybe I see your wounds or maybe I don't.
Either way, I disregard the reality that we are all wounded. All of us.
My ignorance breeds judgmental self-righteousness
        not acceptance.

Love's Goal Is Healing

Love heals; ignorance harms.
There is no neutrality.
Every intention, every thought, every action either heals or harms.
For example, the simple act of brushing one's teeth
    is an act of healing.
One is demonstrating love by caring for one's health.
To skip brushing one's teeth is an act of harm;
    neglecting healthy daily habits that improve life.

Every single thing we do is either a "yes" or a "no"
    to the healing power of love.
If I ignore this fact, I think, speak, or act in ways that hurt others
    and ultimately hurt myself.
I put others down in order to feel superior.
This self-centered and self-serving behavior hurts
    and only contributes to the wounding of the world.

Developing an open heart requires us to face our ignorance—
    to seek out the places where it can fester
    and work to remove it.
This is heart action because it is hearts that change, not heads.

One will not lessen one's hatred or prejudice through analysis.
Change occurs when we understand
    that we are interconnected to all creation,
    that your wounds are just like my wounds,
    that vulnerability is not weakness
        but a truly courageous act,
    that the Divine is Union and that Union is Love.
As we open our hearts more, love increases.
As love increases, our hearts open further.

Love Starts With The Self

I can only love you as much as I love myself.
The degree to which I love myself
    is the degree to which I love others.
When I am wounded, my heart is not fully open.
    In my defensive protection, I will not let you into my heart.
When I can identify my woundedness
    I can tend to those wounds with healing love.
Then, and only then, can I open my heart more fully.

Ruthless compassion is a Buddhist phrase
    referring to the depth of our love.
The definition of the adjective "ruthless" is brutal, cold, pitiless.
How can that adjective be paired with the word "love"?
The reason is because authentic love is ruthless.
When I seek the best for another,
    I must be completely, candidly
    indeed ruthlessly honest.

We struggle with this in our society
    often choosing to be "nice" rather than truthful.
But saying what the other person wants to hear is not love.

It is not love to give another what he or she wants
    if those wants are not in accordance
        with his or her highest good.
And one's highest good is always rooted in truth.

For example, it is not love if a parent spoils his or her child
    by buying everything the child wants.
It's neglecting to teach limitations and sacrifice.
It is not love if a partner always acquiesces to the other's requests.
    It's being submissive in power [third chakra]
        and is not authentic love [fourth chakra].
To tell someone what he or she wants to hear
    instead of the truth is not love.
It's lying.
We often choose to lie because it's scary
    to be ruthlessly compassionate.
Love demands adult actions:
    rigorous honesty,
    strong boundaries,
      courageous vulnerability,
      clear intentions that needs supersede wants.

Love in Action
Service is the spiritual practice of love through helping each other.
Christianity's Jesus of Nazareth offers an exemplary view of love
    in the parable of the Good Samaritan, [Luke 10: 25]
A lawyer asks Jesus how to gain eternal life.
Jesus responds with the Shema:
    "You shall love the Lord your God
    with all your heart, with all your soul, with all your strength
    and love your neighbor as yourself."
But the lawyer presses Jesus: "Who is my neighbor?"

Using a simple parable, Jesus confronts
    the legalistic closed-heartedness of his people
    by telling the story of a man beaten by robbers
    and left for dead.
A priest and a Levite pass by but do not help.
Then a Samaritan finds the victim, bandages him,
    takes him to an inn,
    and pays for his recovery.

Most interpret this parable's message as a command
    to help those in need.
That is certainly part of the point.
There is a sharper r point Jesus is making.
    Why do the priest and Levite pass by?
    Why do they not help the fallen man?
Priests in first century Judaism were "ministers of the Lord"
    and in charge of Temple sanctity.
Levites [descendants of Levi, one of the Twelve Tribes of Israel]
    assisted the priests.
Both are important men in the community, dedicated to God.
So why aren't they the heroes of the story?

The initial interpretation is
    that they put the law above service to the individual.

The victim of this robbery is probably bleeding
> possibly even dying.

According to Jewish law, touching blood
> or a dead body renders one unclean.

If they were ritually contaminated,
> neither the priest nor the Levite could enter the Temple
> to do their jobs until after purification.

They walk past, putting the law first
> refusing to put their jobs in jeopardy
> for an injured stranger.

A deeper interpretation is that perhaps Jesus' audience
> is just as shocked as we are that the priest and the Levite
> are not the compassionate champions of the story.

Perhaps Jesus' point is to jolt them into understanding love's depths.

In the previous chapter of Luke 9: 51,
> Jesus and the disciples try to secure lodging
> in a Samaritan town but they are not welcome.

Reacting in anger, James and John ask,
> "Lord, do you want us to call down fire from the heavens
> to consume them?"

Like the vast majority of humanity when rejected and disrespected,
> the disciples wanted to respond with violence.

So when the lawyer presses Jesus with the question
> "Who is my neighbor?",
> Jesus seizes the opportunity to teach both
> > the lawyer and his disciples.

His lesson has a twist that both shocks and confronts his audience.
The two people that Jesus' listeners expect to be heroes are not.
Rather, the champion of love is
> an unwelcome and disliked Samaritan.

There are four vital lessons from the Samaritan's behavior.
First, he helps an outsider.
> Samaritans and the Jews of Israel were bitter rivals.
> For one to help the other was extraordinary.

Second, the Samaritan does not judge or blame the beaten man;
> he simply helps him.

Third, the Samaritan acts in the best interest of the injured man.
> The wounded man's needs supersede
> the wants of the Samaritan.

Fourth, he expects no recompense or gratitude
> for his act of service.
> > He doesn't seek fame or reward or a medal.

One can imagine the audience being shocked.
After all, no one expects his or her enemy to be heroic.
But that is the measure and message of compassion:
> to love your neighbors and your enemies as yourself
> > to eliminate judgment of the victim
> > to act for the highest good of another
> > and to do so without expecting recompense or applause.

Jesus' command to the lawyer is love's command to us:
> "Go and do likewise."

Forgiveness

Forgiveness is the act of voluntarily and intentionally
        releasing one's feelings of being hurt
        or victimized in order to heal.
It is an act of compassion and clemency.
For Rev. Martin Luther King, forgiveness is a catalyst
        creating the atmosphere necessary for a fresh start.

There are two levels to forgiveness.
A. We all incur karma when we hurt another.
When we forgive, we can release the other person
        from the karma they incurred.
This does not mean the person will get to escape
        learning his/her lessons;
        the lessons remain, but the karma is absolved.

This is the path of forgiveness I took with my parents.
I could not be in relationship with my parents
        but I could release them
        of all karma they incurred during my childhood.

This took me years and by the time I was ready to forgive
        both my parents were deceased.
But whether they were living or dead was irrelevant
        because forgiven transcends all realms.
Talking to my parents' spirits
        I released them from their karma.

B. The second level of forgiveness is that we release karma
        and rebuild the relationship.
We allow healing to replace the pain
        so that the bond that was broken can be restored.

This type of forgiveness happened frequently when I was married.
My partner and I would argue, fight, say hurtful things,
        and forgive each other, restoring our relationship.

Forgiveness does not mean ignoring what has been done;
        it is not repackaging evil with kind words;
        it is not instantaneous;
        it cannot be ordered or coerced or bribed or demanded;
        it is not agreeing the event that happened
            was moral, ethical, or healthy;
        it is never a sign of weakness.
Forgiveness requires courage and strength.

Forgiveness means that the event that caused the break
        is no longer a block or an obsession.
The act is reconstructed, rehabilitated, restored, or purged.
Forgiveness means that the act is no longer a barrier for us.

For decades I hated myself.
As I healed, I began to understand that part of the hatred was
        that I could not forgive myself—
            forgive myself for surviving,
            for healing from the abuse,

            for trying to be authentic,
            for loving myself and seeking wholeness.
I felt tremendous fear, shame, and guilt for surviving.

The learning that followed these insights was monumental:
        forgiving others was optional,
        forgiving myself was mandatory.
The first person I needed to make amends to was me
        for my self-hatred and my self-destructive behaviors.

Love demands we reflect on our intentions, attitudes, and actions
          to discover where we have hurt ourselves or others.
Then we must forgive ourselves for our shortcomings.
No matter what we did, self-hatred, guilt, and shame
        are not the path to wholeness.
Forgiving ourselves and learning our lessons are mandatory.

Forgiving others is optional, dependent upon many factors.
The following outline some of the difficulties we face
        in forgiving others.

A. I don't forgive out of self-righteous indignation.
I'm right; the other person is wrong.
I was hurt; the other person owes me an apology.
Yes, that all that might be true, but...
        this is really ego motivated and an abuse of power.

B. I don't forgive out of resentment.
I am hurt and want the other person to pay in some fashion.
This is a dangerous position that can easily lead to
        rage, revenge, violence, or stupidity.
If I pursue this course of action
        I will inevitably end up with a closed and hardened heart.

C. I don't forgive because I hurt too much.
This is legitimate reason for not forgiving someone.
But don't bask in your self-pity and pain.
The person who hurt you may not be able or available to heal you;
        the task of healing is yours.

This is where I was for years as I dealt with my abuse.
I was horrifically hurt and by their refusal
        to admit the abuse happened.
My parents were not emotionally or spiritually available to me.

D. I conditionally forgive because I want a certain outcome.
A common example is bartering forgiveness for love:
        If I forgive you, you will love and stay with me
        in this relationship.
This is not real forgiveness but another abuse of power.
Genuine forgiveness is from the heart
        without strings or expectations.

As you consider whether to forgive or not
        each situation is judged on its own merits.
After examining the relationship, your needs, and your chords,
        you can make a decision that is healthy
        and seeks your highest good.

4TH FUNDAMENTALS

4th Chakra Basics

Location	From bottom of the rib cage to tops of the shoulders including the arms, hands and fingers
Color	Green
Religion	Christianity
Governs	1. Open-heartedness
	2. Chords
	3. Seat of the soul
	4. Service

1. Open-heartedness

The point of life is to walk in the world with an open heart.
This is compassion; this is love when
  one is openly appreciative and empathic to all creation.
It is the intention, attitude, and behavior
  of seeking the highest good,
  of choosing what is best for one's self and another.

Love is the zenith of our humanity—
  the summit of our actions and efforts.
It is the place of affinity, where an allowance to "be" is our creed
  and we love others and ourselves as we are.[54]

When the fourth chakra is open, I am love,
  being compassionate and acceptable to all,
    even those I don't like.
I maintain healthy boundaries, so my love is pure,
  seeking what is best for myself and the other.
It is not my ego that motivates me
  but a sincere desire to assist both of us
    in gaining our greatest good.

When the fourth chakra is compromised,
  I avoid vulnerability by being:
  distant, withdrawn   [shutting others out]
  defensive or aggressive   [not trusting others to be close]
  bitter, angry, resentful [blaming others]

Love is the action of seeing others as ourselves;
  when we cannot do that we close our hearts in fear.
Sometimes I am unable to see you as me out of self-righteousness:
  I believe I am right and you are wrong.

Sometimes I am unable to see you as me out of jealousy:
  I feel I am lacking and that leads to resentment and envy.
Sometimes I am unable to see you as me
  because you mirror back to me the characteristics
    I don't like about myself.
That glaring image of my own shortcomings
  is too difficult for me to embrace
    so I close my heart to you.
Love is a frightening act of vulnerability.

---

[54] Bergeson

Sometimes we refuse to risk being open-out of fear of getting hurt.
We sidestep an exposed heart
>> build walls to insulate it
>> >> and function primarily out of our intellect.

I did this for years.
I used rational and analytical thinking, staying safely in my head,
>> believing I was acting out of love
>> >> when I really was acting out of unemotional logic.
Now there is nothing wrong with logic
>> but by definition, it pertains to a rational proof.
And love is not rational or logical or intellectual.
It is the passion and power of the spirit.
When we are functioning with a split between our heart and head,
>> we come across as numb or frozen;
>> respond intellectually to emotional situations,
>> express the same emotion or very few emotions.

Bluntly put, I am living in falsehood when there is a split
>> between my head and my heart
>> because I am not connected to my soul.
There can be no major changes in my life—no real change—
>> because the heart is what changes, not the head.
The wall I built for protection has isolated my heart
>> not only from others but from myself.

Authentic love means:
>> wanting the best for you
>> >> but not being your doormat or your savior;
>> helping you get what you need, not everything you want;
>> being ruthless in speaking the truth;
>> and expecting the same from you.
This makes love a very vulnerable act.
Hence the only way to love well is
>> to create and maintain healthy boundaries.

Boundaries

Boundaries are setting limits
>> so that you remain senior in your space.
They are invisible, energetic fences with layers of intimacy.
Strong, conscientious boundaries allow us
>> to have our hearts more open.

These fences vary depending on the relationship.
A useful diagram to illustrate boundaries is the "bull's eye".
"A" as center with rings extending outward.

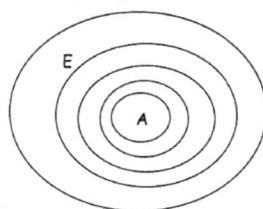

A. You, your soul, your spiritual helpers, God.
>> No other person should be in this place.

B. Your significant other, your most intimate relationship.

C. Your closest friends, teachers, therapist, family
        This is the place for those you confidentially trust

D. Your friends and acquaintances

E. Strangers

While this bull's eye helps demonstrate general boundaries,
        within these relationships, we will have specific limits.
A good analogy for different kinds of boundaries is that of fencing.
With those I trust, my boundaries may be like a short picket fence:
        a separating obstacle that is not very restrictive
        or confining.
My friends may walk up to it, know when to stop, and can chat over it.
Due to the pickets, friends see through it
        and if I am need or want them to,
        they may cross it.

On the other extreme, those I don't trust may encounter my wall:
        thick, solid, high, impermeable.
No one will miss the obviousness and certainty of this barrier
        nor will anyone scale circumvent, or overcome it.

No matter what type of fencing we use, consciousness is vital
        so our boundaries are appropriate for our highest good.
Boundaries are choices we make and set.
Like good fences, they can be moved, re-enforced, or removed—
        multiple times at our request.

Clues that our boundaries have been compromised or lost include:
lose your certainty about what to do or how to proceed;
        can't disagree with someone;
        feel ashamed;
feel you are a bad person;
feel you have done something wrong;
        are persuaded to changed your mind
                when you really don't want to;
you say "yes" when you need to say "no"';

If you find you can't disagree with someone
        or you are giving an answer you really don't want to give,
        you are seeing faces from your past.
Face the triggered memory in order to move forward in adulthood.

If you start to see a pattern of losing your boundaries with someone
        you are probably losing them in the same place
        with everybody.
Don't lose heart.
We all lose our boundaries.
It's part of learning how to be in relationship as an adult.

Resetting Boundaries Techniques
There are several techniques that help us to regain our boundaries.
A. Reclaim your space and reclaim your seniority.
Say "No and Goodbye" with affinity to all energies

that are not yours.
Remember if you are getting run by another energy
    and lose your seniority,
        you are agreeing to that energy on some level.
Reset your intention and examine your fears.

B. Name the loss of boundary.
Naming the issue helps to separate it from yourself.
For example, when I feel I get tempted to open the ice cream,
    I say out loud, "Hi Temptation."
That identification helps me ask myself
    if eating ice cream at this moment is not what I really need.

C. Figure out exactly what happened.
Is this my problem?
If not, whose?
What is my lesson in this?

D. Physically move the energy you don't want out of your body:
Cry,
Scream,
Talk.

Do an energetic body wipe-off by using your hands
    to brush your entire body
Send the energy to Mother Earth.

Whatever method you choose
    do not isolate it, deny it happened, or freeze your energy.

E. Give the person back his or her energy.
Say with affinity, "[person's name], take this energy.
It is yours and not mine. I give it back to you."

F. Ground into Neutrality.
Neutrality is just that—the ability to be neutral impartial.
It is the ability to be in the middle
    between feeling nothing and feeling everything.
Neutrality is very useful when listening or reading another
    so you don't engage in the other person's issues.

Steps to Neutrality:
    Ground.
    Go to the "neutral" of emotion.
Do this by envisioning total happiness then total boredom.
    Then find the middle between these two.

2. Chords
Chords are energetic connections to something or someone else.
As adults, we choose to give and receive love.
The bonds of those relationships are called chords.

Children are especially vulnerable in the fourth chakra
    because they cannot keep out others' energy.
They do not have enough ego strength or maturity to
    differentiate between love and manipulation.

This is important because we may still have chords from childhood
    that are inappropriate, unnecessary, or unhealthy for us.
In some chakras, chords are appropriate and necessary
    but in some chakras, chords are improper and unhealthy.
Chords are proper in the second, fourth, fifth, and sixth chakras.
    In those chakras, we work with others interdependently.
Chords to others are improper in the first, third, and seven chakras.

Chords in your first chakra indicate
    you are depending on others for your survival.
As an adult, you are fully responsible for your existence
    and the quality of your life.

This does not mean we don't need others.
    It means those chords should never be in the first chakra.

If you have chords in your third, you are being drained
    and someone is sucking off your energy.
Someone is controlling your daily habits
    and how you put yourself into the world.

Love is the action of the fourth chakra.
Conditional love is never a fourth chakra issue;
    it always originates and resides in the third chakra
    as an aspect of dominating power.
If you feel conditional love
    the chord will be in the third chakra not the fourth.

Chords in your seventh chakra indicate that
    others are controlling your relationship with the Divine.
Some religious leaders in strict or authoritarian denominations
    have sought to control their congregants
    by energetically blocking the seventh with a cap.
This often will severely limit the person's ability
    to access the Universe.

If you sense your connection to God is difficult
    set your intention on clearing your seven of all obstacles.
Trust your ability to develop
    and maintain your own relationship with the Divine.

If you find chords in your first, third, or seventh chakras
    ground, clear your chakras, and re-claim your seniority
    or try any other resetting boundary technique.

Within the fourth chakra
    the location of the chord provides information.
Chords in the front of the body indicate
    present, active relationship chords.
Chords in the back of the body indicate past life or dead chords.
Dead chords are attachments to relationships that are long over.

The condition of the chord indicates the state of the connection:
Strong relationships will have resilient and vibrant chords.
Worn out or struggling relationships will have weak
    or frayed chords.
Once you know the status of a chord
    you can decide what you need to do for your own health:

strengthen the chord, release the chord, or do nothing.
To strengthen a chord, one needs to increase intention and action.
Commit to an intention of reinforcing this particular chord,
    seeking the highest good for yourself and the other.
Set your intention freely in compassion;
    love is your guide then let go of the outcome.

Do actions that need to be done to strengthen the chord:
    be more attentive, communicate more,
        change your behavior, etc.
Remember you are not in control of the other person's response.
Ultimately you will have to accept his or her level of participation.

No matter how much you strengthen a chord
    your energy alone cannot make the relationship flourish.
You can keep your chord strong
    and continue to send your energy to the other,
    but that person remains free to accept or reject the chord.

If you decide you need to break a chord,
    do this with neutrality and affinity.
Visualize tying off the chord gently yet firmly.
I picture tying a knot around a cable.
I pull the knot tight until the knot cuts
    and divides the cable into two parts.
Thus the chord is severed.
Then in neutrality and with compassion, I seal the cut ends.
I give the other person back his or her energy
    and I pull my energy to me.

Some clues that it may be time to end a relationship:
    the relationship takes more energy
        than you want to expend;
    the other person has already broken chords with you;
    the relationship is unhealthy
        and the other person is not willing to change;
    the energy for building the relationship is absent.
Remember you can always re-chord if the dynamics change.

Community Chords are connections between groups,
    such as family, club, sports team, particular church, etc.
These features indicate the chords with these groups are healthy:
    sense of "common unity";
    ability to negotiate and compromise;
    common good emphasized
        with individual ways of achieving goals;
    discussion and disagreement are encouraged;
    free will is respected;
    ability to enter and leave at will;
    value people over ideology.

If the group has these features, chords will be less healthy:
    common good with one person deciding
        how to achieve goals
    one person decides when others can join or leave;
    no negotiation wanted;
    free will is not respected and therefore diminished;
    little discussion and no disagreement;

value ideology over people.
Just as with individual relationships,
> one can strengthen or break chords with communities.

3. Seat Of The Soul

Seat of the soul is the fourth chakra little behind
> and above the heart.[85]

Also called, "the place of God", this is where the spiritual becomes
> physical and the physical becomes spiritual.

Energetically, it's where the soul connects to the body.
This is home.
This is where you are a fully alive human person.

4. Service

Service is love in action.
And compassion demands action.
This is the level of being love to the world.

Rabbi Avi Lazerson teaches that there are seven levels of charity.[86]

VII.   One gives grudgingly. [Lowest level of charity]
VI.   One gives less than is proper, but willingly.
V.   One gives upon being asked.
IV.   One gives without being asked.
III.   The giver knows the receiver
>   but the receiver does not know the giver.
II.   One gives in secret:
>   the giver does not know the receiver,
>   the receiver does not know the giver.
I.   One gives to help sustain a person
>   before he or she becomes impoverished
>   by offering a gift in a dignified manner.
>   [Highest level of charity]

Wherever you are on the scale, try to move to the next level.
Despite the balance of your financial accounts,
> there are multiple ways to be generous and open-hearted.

A. Alms-giving is giving money or materials to those in need.
Consider cleaning out your closets, cupboards, and garage.
Whatever items you have not used in the past year, give away.

B. Blessings are an expression of love
> sending forth compassion and energy to others.

Create a short blessing for the world.
Consider these categories:
> family, local, state, country, international;
> ethnic, religious, cultural, social groups;
> health of the body: those who suffer from poverty,
>> homelessness, addiction, torture, disease, illness, war;
> health of the heart: those who suffer from grief, abuse;
> health of the soul: those who suffer from stagnation, fear,
> paralysis, despair.

C. Good deeds are random acts of kindness
> such as a friendly word, needed hug, warm greeting,
> shared treat, listening presence.

---

[85] Judith, 47.
[86] The Rambam on Charity, http://www.jewishmag.com/60mag/charity/charity.htm December. 5, 2014).

D. Healing is a power in all creation.
We tend to underestimate our power to heal.
Offer healing touch or intentions with the conviction
        that you have the power to be a conduit
            for the Divine to heal.

E. Prayer is an excellent act of generosity to others.
Like all acts of service, we must scrutinize our personal motives
        for hidden agendas.
Prayer is a request for God to act.[57]
But how do we want God to act?

Often we pray for a specific goal
        such as "God, heal my sister of cancer."
In that prayer, I am asking for what I believe is the best for my sister.
But how do I know what's best for my sister?
        Do I truly know what my sister needs?

Prayer is not a technique to change God's mind
        but it is a releasing of God's power
            through ourselves in a relationship of cooperation
                with God.[58]
In this relationship with God, I must acknowledge
        my limited vision and finite understanding.
I do not know God's will for my sister or anyone else—
        sometimes not even myself!
Adult prayer must reflect the limits of my knowledge.

Prayer must always yield to God's will.
When my sister was fighting cancer and later dying from it,
        I tried to pray that she be open
            to receiving what she needed
            having absolute confidence
                that the Divine would provide all she required.

F. Volunteer with an organization.
Offer your presence and expertize to a cause you believe it.
Regardless of what type of service you choose
        we become the Samaritan to the world.
We help the wounded, without judgment or feelings of superiority,
        without expectation of repayment
This is the meaning of love.

G. Tithing literally means "one-tenth" and is the term
        for sharing one-tenth of one's gifts and resources.
It is the act of giving back from our abundance.
No matter how much or little we may have, we are asked to share it.

When I was younger, I was frugal and stingy.
I did not believe in sharing
        because I felt like I had so little
        and did not want to share it.
I justified my stinginess by
        believing that my employer was already cheating me
            out of a just salary so I did not need to give any of it back.

---

[57] Stanley Grenz, Prayer: A Cry For The Kingdom, (Grand Rapids, MI: Wm Erdmans Publishing, 2005), 27.
[58] Kenneth Leech, True Prayer, (Harrisburg, PA: Morehouse Publishing, 1995), 25.

When I started to become more generous, I started small—
    at two percent of my gross salary.
Each year I try to increase a percentage point.
Soon I was giving more freely and more open-heartedly.
And tithing became almost fun.
I created a system for choosing the causes I wanted to support
    and thus began to feel empowered and empowering.

Most spiritual traditions encourage sharing.

TRADITION	WORD FOR SERVICE	DEFINITION
NATIVE AMERICAN	Okiçiyapi "to help another" [Dakota]	This is the way of life. Community is primary.
BUDDHISM	Pha "payment from the heart"	The ability and the attitude in the perfection of generosity
ISLAM	Zakat "purification and growth"	Traditionally, 1/40 of one's possessions each year
CHRISTIANITY	Stewardship "just managment of resources"	10% is suggested: 5% to one's church 5% to charity
JUDIASM	Tithing "sharing one-tenth of resources"	10% of one's gross income per year

4th Synopsis
When the fourth chakra is compromised, I am closed-hearted.
I neither give freely nor share easily.
My boundaries are either non-existent or impenetrable.
When my fourth chakra is blocked, I don't feel love.

When the fourth chakra is open and healthy
    I am compassionate to myself and to others.
I have conscientious and appropriate boundaries.
Because I value the relationship chords in life,
    I strive to maintain strong, genuine relationships.
My soul is at home and I work to heal

4th PRACTICES

Read the Fourth Chakra
Read the strengths of the fourth chakra.
Read your chest. What do you see? Hear? Feel? Know?
Read your shoul What do you see? Hear? Feel? Know?
Read your arms to fingers. What do you see? Hear? Feel? Know?
Read your heart. What do you see? Hear? Feel? Know?
What are the strengths of your fourth chakra?
Celebrate the strengths and power of your fourth chakra.

Read for the blocks in the fourth chakra.
Read your chest. Gleam lessons from your blocks.
Read your shoulders. Gleam lessons from your blocks.
Read your arms, hands, fingers. Gleam lessons from your blocks.
Read your heart. Gleam lessons from your blocks.
Do you perceive any patterns Gleam lessons from them.

Read for Faith, Hope, Love
Faith is confidence in something without viable proof.
Hope is courageous trust that all is unfolding as it should.
Love is empathetic acceptance and compassion.
All reside in the fourth chakra.

Read what you know about Faith, Hope, and Love.
Read your level of each one by the gauge of "High/Medium/Low".
You can raise levels by intention
without need of explanation or reason.

Read for Boundaries
Read your boundaries regarding the bull's eye.
Consider your inner and outer circles.
Are they healthy for you?
Where are your boundaries weak or lost?
How can you strengthen them?

Practice Neutrality
Ground. Go to the "neutral" of emotion.
Do this by envisioning total happiness then total boredom.
Then find the middle between these two.

A Variety of Cleansing Techniques
Say "No / Goodbye"
Put on glass body
Bathe in sea salt
Sage your body and space

Take mini-vacation above your seventh chakra
Cleanse with cedar
Do something to keep you in present time and space
Ask guides, angels, healers, and helpers for assistance
Wipe off your arms, hands, legs, feet, etc.
        and give that energy to earth

Germ's Litany Of The Saints
Response: Teach us.

Black Elk, who heard the voice and listened...
Siddhartha, who entered the silence to find truth...
Esther, who stood against abusive power
        for the liberation of her people...
Elizabeth of Judea, who recognized the value of a pregnant woman...
Muhammad, passionate fighter for justice and mercy...
Mary of Magdala, minister to Jesus, apostle to the apostles...
Bridget of Ireland, revered judge and bishop...
Anthony, founder of lost items, desires, and dreams...
Francis of Assisi, first environmentalist in the church...
Rumi, writer of love poems to God...
John of the Cross, mystic, dreamer, and visionary...
Dorothy Day, who led the church to embrace the poor...
Oscar Romero, champion of the dignity of all people...
Gandhi, who challenged the world to become whole...
All holy women and men of God...
Amen!

The Four Limitless Ones Chant[59]
"May all sentient beings enjoy happiness and the root of happiness.
May they be free from suffering and the root of suffering.
May they not be separated from the great happiness
        devoid of suffering.
May they dwell in the seat of equanimity,
        free from passion, aggression, and prejudice."

Prayer when one asks for prayers
A. "May God grant you what you need today."
B. "We lift you up as a whole and holy child of God."[60]
C. "I pray that you are on the path to your greatest good."

Read For Open-Heartedness
Every day read your heart.
Observe where your heart is open.
        How do you manifest your open heart?
Observe where your heart is closed.
        Who are you closed to?
How do you manifest your closed heart?
        Do you want to open your heart more?
Who are your enemies today?
How can you increase your compassion for them?

---

[59] Pema Chodron, The Places That Scare You, (Boston, MA: Shambhala, 2002), 129.
[60] Martha Rowlett, Praying Together, (Nashville, TN: Upper Room, 2002).

Read for Chords
Read for chords in your first, third, and seventh,
If you find chords, examine whose chorded to you and why.
Release the chords you choose with affinity.
Read for chords in your second, fourth, fifth, sixth, and seventh.
Check each chakra to see to whom you are chorded.
What is the condition of the chord?
Is this chord what I want or need today?
Read for community chords.
> Are they healthy and life-giving for you?

Expand Your Prayer Schedule
Enhance and extend your prayer schedule.
If you pray twice a day, try three times a day;
> if four times, try to make it five.

Spread your prayer throughout the day
> to increase consciousness and connection.

Blessings For The Day
God of all creation, bless me with your strength and grace.
I offer my day, my intentions, and my actions for:

Monday	I pray for health and healing of all creation.
Tuesday	May all be awakened to consciousness.
Wednesday	May I walk in my authentic power, with integrity.
Thursday	I pray for all who love me and all who refuse to love me.
Friday	May I communicate today with ruthless compassion.
Saturday	May I continue opening my gifts of intuition.
Sunday	May all creation be one with the Divine.

Loving Ages Practice
Picture yourself at birth.
> Wrap that part of you in unconditional love.

Picture yourself at age five, just starting school.
> Wrap that part of you in unconditional love.

Picture yourself at thirteen, being a teenager.
> Wrap that part of you in unconditional love.

Picture yourself at twenty-five, out in the world.
> Wrap that part of you in unconditional love.

Picture yourself at your present age.
> Wrap that part of you in unconditional love.

Read for Forgiveness
Read where you have forgiven yourself.
> What was your process for doing so?

Read where you are still struggling to forgive yourself.
> What is the issue?
> What is preventing you from forgiving yourself?

Read where you are withholding forgiveness from others.
> Do this objectively without harshness to yourself.

Remember forgiving others does not mean
    you have to be in relationship.
Examine your motives.

Read where you need to make amends.
This is an essential step as there is no escape from karma.
We all hurt others, intentionally and unintentionally.
Adulthood requires we fix what we have broken
    to the best of our ability.
"Make a list of all persons you have harmed
    and become willing to make amends to them all."[61]
Then make amends to all whenever possible
    except when to do so would hurt them or others.[62]

Read for Service
Read for your willingness to serve others.
Examine your resistance and its motives.
A. What in your house do you no longer need or use?
    Consider house-cleaning and giving away items.

B. Do you offer blessings to others?
    Especially those who irritate or anger you?

C. Commit to doing a good deed for someone every day.

D. Offer healing energy today.

E. Expand the scope of your prayers:
    lengthen the prayer itself, add an additional prayer,
    pray for an additional cause, group, or condition.

F. How much do you tithe?
    Consider small incremental increases up to ten percent.
    How do you determine what causes you will support?

H. What causes do you volunteer with?

Primary Prayer from Each Tradition
NATIVE AMERICAN   Ancient Ojibwe prayer
O Great Spirit, whose voice I hear in the winds
    and whose breath gives life to the world, hear me!
I am small and weak.
I need your strength and wisdom.
Let me walk in beauty
    and make my eyes ever behold the red and purple sunset.
May my hands respect the things you have made
    and my ears sharp to hear your voice.
Make me wise so that I may understand
    the things you have taught my people.
Let me learn the lesson you have hidden
    in every leaf and rock.
I seek strength.
Not to be greater than my brother but to fight my greatest enemy—
    myself.
Make me always ready to come to you
    with clean hands and straight eyes.
So when life fades, I may come to you without shame.[63]

---

[61] Alcoholics Anonymous, 59.
[62] Alcoholics Anonymous, 59.
[63] Jones, 170.

BUDDHISM   Ancient Buddhist chant
By this merit may all obtain omniscience.
May it defeat the enemy wrong-doing.
From the stormy waves of birth, old-age, sickness and death,
From the ocean of Samsara may I free all beings.

ISLAM   Fatiha, first sura in the Qur'an
In the name of God, the Compassionate and the Merciful.
Praise be to God, Lord of all the worlds,
        most Compassionate, most Merciful.
Ruler on the Day of Reckoning.
You alone do we worship, and You alone do we ask for help.
Guide us on the straight path,
        the path of those who have received your grace;
        not the path of those who have brought down wrath,
        nor of those who wander astray. Amen."

CHRISTIANITY   Prayer of Francis of Assisi
Lord, make me an instrument of Your peace.
Where there is hatred let me sow love;
        where there is injury, pardon;
        where there is doubt, faith;
        where there is despair, hope;
        where there is darkness, light;
        where there is sadness, joy.
O, Divine Master, grant that I may not so much seek
        to be consoled as to console;
        to be understood as to understand;
        to be loved as to love;
For it is in giving that we receive;
        it is in pardoning that we are pardoned;
        it is in dying that we are born again to eternal life."

JUDAISM   Shema, Deuteronomy 6: 4-7
Hear, O Israel, the Lord is our God, the Lord is One.
Blessed be the name of the glory of His kingdom forever and ever.
You shall love the Lord your God with all your heart,
        with all your soul, and with all your might.
And these words which I command you today
        shall be upon your heart.
You shall teach them thoroughly to your children,
        and you shall speak of them when you sit in your house
        and when you walk on the road
        when you lie down and when you rise.

HINDUISM   A favorite of Mohandas Gandhi
O Thou dweller in my heart,
        open it, purify it, make it bright and beautiful.
Awaken it, prepare it, make it fearless.
Make it a blessing to others.
Rid it of laziness, free it from doubt.
Make my heart fixed on You
and make it full of joy, full of joy, full of joy.[64]

Loving Kindness Practice[65]

Loving Kindness Practice is a method of healing those we love
        and those we don't love.

---

[64] Mohandas Gandhi, Book of Prayers, (Berkeley CA: Berkley Hill, 1999), 109.
[65] Pema Chodron, Session Two 2.6, "Awakening Love", Jan 13 – Mar 6, 2011, audio tape, Sound Tunes, Gampo Abbey, Cape Breton, Nova Scotia, 2012.

TRADITIONAL LOVING KINDNESS PRACTICE
Start with love for yourself
Picture yourself as happy, resting at peace;
    let your heart open to yourself.

Say for yourself, "May I enjoy happiness & the root of happiness.
    May I be free from suffering and the root of suffering
        craving, aggression, and prejudice.
    May I dwell in equanimity, the place of fullness of being."
For a loved one.
Picture soft, loving, white light ,
    extending from your heart to a loved one
    letting that light surround them from head to toe.

Say for a loved one
    "May you enjoy happiness and the root of happiness.
    May you be free from suffering and the root of suffering
        cravings, aggression, and prejudice.
    May you dwell in equanimity, the place
        of fullness of being."

Repeat for a stranger.

Repeat for a difficult person.

Picture yourself from the sky, looking at the entire world
Say for all creation
    "May all creation enjoy happiness
        and the root of happiness.
    May all creation be free from suffering
        and the root of suffering:
        cravings, aggression, prejudice.
    May all creation dwell in equanimity
        the place of fullness of being."

ALTERNATIVE LOVING KINDNESS PRACTICE
Picture yourself as happy, resting at peace;
    let your heart open to yourself.
Say "May I enjoy physical, emotional, mental, spiritual well-being.
    May I dwell in deepest well-being"

Say for loved one
    "May you enjoy physical happiness and good health.
    May you enjoy emotional well-being
        and a harmonious life.
    May you enjoy mental happiness and peace of mind.
    May you enjoy spiritual happiness
        and wholeness of being.
    May you dwell in deepest well-being"

Repeat for stranger.

Then repeat for a difficult person.

Picture yourself from the sky, looking at the entire world
Say for all creation, 'May all creation open more and more each day.
    May all creation be free from patterns and habits
        that shut down openness.
    May all creation work to heal the world.
    May all creation dwell in deepest well-being."

Tonglen Word Meditation

Using a string of beads, meditate on a particular word
        as you count off the beads with your fingers.
I chose to use the 108 beads of Hinduism
        108 symbolizing the entire universe.

DATE	LETTER	POSSIBLE	CHOICES
1	A	Avoidance/Acceptance	Arrogance/Authentic
2	B	Boredom/Boldness	Boastful/Beauty
3	C	Cynicism/Commitment	Cruelty/Courage
4	D	Dishonesty/Dignity	Doubt/Dedication
5	E	Enraged/Enlightenment	Egotism/Essence
6	F	Fear/Fortitude	Foolish/Faith
7	G	Grumpiness/Gentleness	Greed/Generosity
8	H	Harshness/Happiness	Harmfulness/Health
9	I	Inflexible/Interdependence	Intolerant/Integrity
10	J	Jealousy/Joy	Jadedness/Justice
11	K	Knotted/Kindness	Keyless/Key
12	L	Loneliness/Love	Limiting/Limitless
13	M	Mean-spiritedness/Mercy	Miserly/Mindfulness
14	N	Negativity/Natural	Noxious/Nurture
15	O	Obsessive/Optimism	Obstinate/Originality
16	P	Pessimism/Positivity	Pessimism/Power
17	Q	Quit/Quintessence	Quarrelsome/Quiet
18	R	Rudeness/Redemption	Resentful/Rejuvenation
19	S	Self-centeredness/Strength	Selfishness/Stillness
20	T	Threatening/Truth	Turbulence/Trust
21	U	Unreliability/Ultimate	Untrustworthy/Unity
22	V	Vulgar/Venerable	Vengeful/Valor
23	W	Wanting/Worthiness	Woundedness/Wonder
24	X	Xenophobia/X	Xenophobia/Xenial
25	Y	Yammer/Yield	Yen/Yield
26	Z	Zilch/Zenith	Zapped/Zeal
27	all enduring abuse		
		Worthlessness/Wholeness	Harming/Healing
28	all suffering from depression		
		Contradictory/Compassion	Hopelessness/Hope
29	all caught in addiction		
		Relapse/Recovery	Sickness/Sobriety
30	all preparing for death		
		Denial/Death	Anxiety/Awakening

Mantras on the Gifts of the 4th Chakra

A. Breathe in "forgiveness"; breathe out "forgiveness".
B. Breathe in "acceptance"; breathe out "empathy".
C. Breathe in "gentleness"; breathe out "interdependence".

4th GIFTS

1. When I walk in the world
      with good boundaries   I am love.

2. When I seek the best for myself
      and others   I am ruthless compassion.

3. When I work to heal the world   I am blessing.

4. When I pray   I am one with God.

5. When I willingly share
      my gifts   I am service.

6. When my soul is in my heart   I am home.

7. When my fourth chakra is open
      with good boundaries   I am.

5. TRUTHFUL COMMUNICATION

PHILOSOPHY OF COMMUNICATION

Communication is the art of connection.
It is the outward expression of identity, honesty, and authenticity.
Whereas grounding is the most important spiritual practice
        communication is the most important social practice.

The goal of communication is to express who we are.
Regardless of how we choose to communicate
        or what we choose to divulge ,
        two vital opportunities always present themselves.
First, some aspect of our identity will be known to another;
        second, we open the door to further self-discovery.
For every time I reveal myself to you, I reveal myself to me also.

Therefore communicating truth is the objective of the fifth chakra.
Truthfulness is vital for walking a spiritual path.
It is the honest and direct stating of what we know at
        this moment to be real.

To be truthful is both a fidelity to the meaning of the words
        and the proper intention to the person
        to whom we are communicating.
"Fidelity to the meaning of the words" is a commitment to the truth
        without being ambiguous or confusing or evasive.
"Proper intention" means our communicative aim
        is to express the truth
without deception by word, by body language, or by silence.
Or simply put: the truth, the whole truth and nothing but the truth.

Speaking truth is a tremendous challenge especially in our culture.
We are bombarded with messages depicting deception
        and lying as standard.

Built For Truth

But we are built for truth.
The Divine and Truth are identical.
In the words of Mohandas Gandhi
        "I have come to the conclusion that God is Truth.
        Two years ago, I went a step further
        and said Truth is God.' [66]
Gandhi's powerful statement speaks
        to the depth and breadth of truth's significance.

Because I believe I am part of God, then I am truth and truth is me.
        To deny truth is to deny my identity, my being.
Hence the cost for being untruthful is quite expensive.
Learning to be truthful is a process.
Our education in truth-telling advances as we recognize
        and examine the motives behind our dishonesty.

The fact is the truth is seldom popular and maybe even dangerous.
Fear is always the chief culprit when we avoid being truthful.
The following outlines some of those fears
        and our motives to be dishonest.

---

[66] Mohandas Gandhi, Essential Writings, (Maryknoll, NY: Orbis Books, 2006), 72.

A. Speaking truth risks punishment, ridicule, or rejection by others.
The strongest motive we have for not telling the truth
       is the fear of punishment.
Whether real or imagined,
       the fear of being in trouble motivates us to lie.
Punishment comes in a multitude of disguises.
What is the price for telling the truth?

If I speak the truth, will you still like me?
Will I be hurt physically?
       [slapped, hit, arrested, imprisoned]
Will I be hurt emotionally?
       [laughed at, discounted]
Will I be hurt socially?
       [outcast from group]
Will I be hurt financially?
       [demoted, fired]

In weighing the costs, the expense of lying is almost always
       greater than the value of truth
       because every time we lie, we sacrifice our very selves.
Dishonesty costs us our integrity and honor.

B. Speaking truth will impact others.
Another looming fear is the mistaken belief
       that our truth can hurt another.
It cannot.
Others may not like our truth.
They may react to it with a host of emotions
       from codependent anger or passive aggression
       to deafening silence.
Their own struggles and issues cause these reactions.

Truth is light.
It illuminates the path for us.
Those who are in darkness fear the light.
Not because the light will hurt them
       but because the light illuminates areas of growth
       inviting them to change.
Light cannot hurt them.

Quite the opposite,
       truth opens a door for all to embrace authenticity.
I cannot control how others react or respond to my truth.
By lying to placate another, I sacrifice authenticity for both of us.

To combat this fear, we need effective communication skills.
The most important is to use "I" language.
Because I want to blame others, I often use "you" statements.
       "You make me so mad. You didn't take out the garbage."

These statements create many additional problems
       because they are accusatory, they promote defensiveness.
They give my power over to the person I am angry at
       and because they give my power away
       I can't own my emotional state.
The result often is a bigger argument, with both sides hurt.

"I" language is honest, authentic,
        and allows me to stand in my power.
        "I am so angry.
        I am so frustrated
        because the garbage is still in the kitchen."
This communication is more effective, less aggressive, and healthier
        when I own what I feel and want.
It builds better conversations which build better relationships.

C. Speaking truth will expose who I really am.
Sometimes dishonesty is rooted in our anxiety
        of being seen in our authenticity.
Especially if we fear our character defects might be laid bare.
Afraid our truth will leave us too vulnerable, we keep secrets.
The challenge of this fear is to distinguish the fine line
        between maintaining privacy and keeping secrets.

As a human being, I have the right to privacy.
But as an adult, secrets tend to kill life.
One must be attuned to the distinction between the two.

For example, as a recovery addict,
        I reveal that truth to those I choose.
Early in my recovery, I was worried about my job security
        if word got out I was an addict
        so I maintained both silence and privacy.
As I grow stronger in my identity, the need for privacy lessens.
When I first began recovery
        I told no one I was an addict; today it's a published fact.

Being silent regarding my addiction
        was my own conscious decision.
I could maintain my privacy because the revelation of my addiction
        has no impact on others.
It is my private life and no one else's business.

But if an employer would ask of my drug history,
        my refusal to divulge my addiction
        has now become a secret.

And this secret can kill me:
        physically because lying puts my recovery in jeopardy,
        emotionally because fear is dictating my behavior,
        spiritually because I have sacrificed my truth.

Keeping secrets hides something that needs
        to be brought into the light.
When I lie to keep the truth secret, I negate my highest good.
Rigorous honesty demands I own my uncompromised truth
        while maintaining privacy with healthy boundaries.

D. Speaking truth negates my control over situations and others.
Being in control is a very tempting motivation for dishonesty—
        we lie to manipulate others so they will act as we want.
This type of lie is the basis of many advertisements.

If you use this shampoo, buy this car, drink this beer,
        you will be loved by all the beautiful people.

If you do not, you're an unpopular and lonely loser.
Being bombarded with this type of manipulation,
        we gravitate toward it in our communications.

However, it is really just another example of our power
        being out of balance.
Whenever I use my words to influence another to act as I desire
        I am manipulative.
This is particularly important in our emotional expression.
It is very tempting and easy to use emotions to manipulate another.

For example, do you cry and express grief
        so that another will take care of you?
Do you take care of another adult
        when she/he appears weak and vulnerable?
Do you get angry in order to motivate another to do what you want?
Do you do what another wants because she/he is angry with you?

The expression of my emotional state is for my benefit.
If my end game is the manipulation of another
        then I am misusing both my power   [third chakra]
        and my truth   [fifth chakra].
When speaking my emotional truth, I am standing in my power
        to name and claim what I feel and who I am.

Honest communication allows for disagreements
        as well as swaying of opinions,
        because truth never manipulates; it empowers.
Using one's passion or convictions
        invites others to either agree with us
        Or discover their own passions and convictions.

Why face all these fears of truth telling?
Because the lying is too expensive.
In lying, there is a contraction, a constriction of energy.
I can feel it in my muscles and organs;
        it is as if my body closes in on itself.
Lies take more energy because:
        lies are fiction, we have to remember them;
        we are more hyper-vigilant in trying to remember them;
        we live in fear of being caught in our lie;
        we know, at a deep level,
        we have compromised our integrity.

In truth-telling, there is an expansion of energy,
        a clarity and clearness throughout my being.
As I speak the truth, I stand taller in my power.
I don't have to rely on my mind to remember—
        every cell in my body knows the truth.
Regardless of another's response to my honesty,
        I am true to myself.

The Truth About Truth

A. The truth leads to wholeness for the speaker of truth.
It doesn't hurt anyone. It simply is.
It is like light, illuminating our path.
There are exceptions to this.

If one were under threat of violence
        one could justify not speaking the truth.

Another exception would be if the truth cannot be comprehended.
My friend relates this example:
"My mom had Alzheimer
        and repeatedly asked me about her younger sister.
My aunt had died and my mom kept forgetting.
Only once did I make the mistake of retelling her truth
        where she had to re-experience the death."[67]
B. Truth is empowering.
Expansive and inviting, the truth opens the door to authenticity.
It is only in truth that one can discover identity and purpose.

C. Truth cannot be possessed.
Throughout history, individuals, governments, and religions
        have mistakenly believed they owned
        and controlled truth.
That path often leads to violence in the name of truth.

The reality is truth cannot be possessed; it must be served.
It is God and as a Higher Power truth demands respect and honor.

D. Truth changes.
As we grow, our truth changes as we become more conscious.
I do not believe the same things I believed ten years ago
        or even ten days ago.
There is a story from Gandhi's life that depicts this so clearly.
After a talk Gandhi gave, a reporter approached him and said,
        "Mr. Gandhi, I was at your talk last week
        and you said the opposite thing then."
Gandhi replied, "It is not my job to be consistent.
        It is my job to be consistent with the truth
        as it presents itself to me."

Gandhi's truth changed with his enlightenment.
That is the gift of truth—
        as we learn more, truth is increasing its light to us.
This is the hope for the world.
No matter where we are on the path
        the opportunity for truth to increase is always present.

E. When we stand facing the mirror
        identity, truth, and authenticity
        are all we are and all we have.
My image, masks, popularity, and possessions
        are all elements outside myself.
What I really possess, the only thing I really possess is who I am.
I am truth and to speak my truth is to declare my wholeness.

---

[67] Mary Mohan, conversation with author June 1, 2015.

5th FUNDAMENTALS

5th Chakra Basics

Location	From the bottom of the neck to base of the skull including the throat, mouth, nose, eyes, and ears
Color	Blue
Religion	Judaism
Governs	1. Communication
	2. Soul tasks and life blueprint
	3. Intuitive abilities

1. Communication

The fifth chakra governs communication in all forms:
    smelling, tasting, seeing, touching,
    listening, speaking, writing and studying.

A. Through the senses the world communicates to us.
Our senses are the communicative tools
    through which we receive information
    to connect with and understand our world.
Samples are easy to find:
    smelling a freshly picked rose, tasting a creamy caramel.
    seeing a sunset full of color, touching a baby's face.
Through our sense, our world communicates
    boundless information to us
    and then we decide how to communicate back.

As we continue to open the fifth chakra
    we will possess greater sensory awareness.
We are more attuned to what we smell, taste, see, and hear
    physically, emotionally, mentally, spiritually.

B. Listening is a mandatory skill in the art of communication.
It is hearing the words as well as the depth of what is said
    so that the other person feels understood.
To truly listen to another is a tremendously valuable gift.
The skill of listening is one of being present
    in a spirit of empathetic respect.

Clues my listening skills are ineffective or unhelpful:
    I react rather than respond;
    I am swayed by the conversation and join in the fight—
        seizing an "us against them" mentality ;
    I know the "right" answer to the problem;
    I formulate my answer while the other person
        is still speaking.

As a good listener, I have the following characteristics:
    I stand in my own power—
    I am not threatened by what I hear;
    I allow the other person to express his/her words
        and emotions without trying to control them;
    I can distinguish between the emotion
        and the reality of the situation;

        I can listen objectively
                without jumping on my own soapbox or judgement.
        I can listen intently without hurrying
                to formulate my response;
        my response is rooted in ruthless compassion.

The twin of listening is, of course, speaking.
The primary role of the fifth chakra is
        to communicate our truth to others
                predominantly using the voice in verbal communication.

While there are many types of truths
        [logical, mathematical, scientific, ontological]
        the most important for adulthood is soul truth.
Soul truth is who I am at my core:
        my worth, my dignity, my value as a human being.
It includes both who I am and what my purpose is for this lifetime.
I seek to communicate to others who I am:
        my identity because I long to be known.
Being known means I am seen as I really am.

Being in relationship with others mirrors back to me who I am.
It's through connection with others
        that I develop and articulate my identity.

The challenge is that all connection is risky.
The first risk focuses on my ability to clearly express who I am.
What if I cannot articulate my identity effectively?
This risk is only overcome with practice.
Yes, there are times I will misspeak
        and my words will be rabbled, scrabbled, and muddled.
The solution is to ground, listen to my truth, and speak again.

The second risk often appears more formidable.
What if "they" don't like who I am?
What if "they" don't accept me as I am?
The risk is great because the risk is rejection.
Especially when we were young, the fear of rejection
        often motivated us to compromise who we were
            in order to fit in.
So we put on masks and pretended to be someone different—
        someone that we think the group wants and likes—
        in an attempt to be part of the group.

But this will always be a futile attempt because we are not our masks
        and the masks are not us.
The price of wearing a mask too long is
        that we may believe the mask is us.
We lose the ability to distinguish this façade from our true selves;
        and the fear of being our true selves
            without the mask grows.
And the full price of that is losing our authenticity.
Masks are the antithesis of being a fully alive human person.

Communication is what links us as humans.
When I relate to others
> I have the opportunity to belong to be part of the group.

We all long for this connection, to be acknowledged, accepted
> and part of something beyond our own individuality.

The challenge of communication is to peel off the mask,
> stand in my authentic self
> to show the world who I really am.

Real communication challenges us to risk the rejection of others
> for the goal of being authentic
> because the essence of real communication is truth.

Only when I honor my truth can I speak my truth
> and only then can I live my truth.

A Word on Words

Our task is to speak the truth with ruthless compassion;
> how we speak that truth is exceedingly important.

Just as it is not necessary to use a sledgehammer on a thumbtack,
> it is not helpful to be harsh, severe, sharp, or tactless.

Before speaking, ask the following:
> Are my words necessary?
> Are my words articulate?
> Are my words tactful?

C. When others communicate with me
> I then learn more fully who I am.

Humans are social beings and learning is a communal act.
> If I read a book, the book is my companion in learning.
> If I listen to the Divine, the Divine is my teacher.

Study is the practice of engaging the mind to transform the heart.
Its goal is not simply to increase knowledge
> but to allow that new knowledge to break down old beliefs
> or patterns in order to continue growth.

Study is not simply the reading of a text but wrestling with it.

We study so that in discovering others' wisdom,
> we increase our own.

This learning does not occur in isolation
> but in relationship with other human beings
> via reading and dialogue.

Judaism is the religion woven to the fifth chakra.
Jewish tradition is rooted in its passion for learning through
> rigorous wrestling with texts, animated verbal sparring,
> dynamic debates and continual education.

In Judaism, the concept of education extends beyond the classroom; it is training for life.
To instill one with the love of learning meant
> that study of religious texts would be
> a life-long adventure.[68]

One's education does not end with the diploma or the ceremony;
> it in fact continues to death.

The principle insight of study is that
> one needs to be challenged by other voices.

Within educational circles,
> Judaism encourages the use of study partners
> to inspire intellectual stimulation

---

[68] George Robinson, Essential Judaism, (New York City, NY: Pocket Books, 2000), 157.

and encourage lively debate.
The point is not to indoctrinate one with the "right" answer
> but to challenge the learner to own his or her own view.

Koens are Buddhist brainteasers.
Typically a teacher would give the student one koen at a time.
The student then wrestles with the meaning of the koen.
Only after asserting the correct answer
> does the student get the next koen.

The point is to think outside the box of conventional reason
> to achieve greater wisdom.

Try this koen. The answer is in the "**5th Practices**" section.
> "If you see the Buddha on the road, kill him."

Play with it; wrestle with it.
Resist the urge to look up the answer.
Challenge yourself to discover the meaning behind the koen.

2. Soul's Task and Life Blueprint

Each person has a purpose for living this life at this time in history.
Called "soul tasks" or "life tasks", they are our primary learnings
> and specific responsibilities this lifetime.

For example, one of my soul tasks this lifetime is to learn
> to recover from sexual abuse.

This probably has been my soul task has for lifetimes.
This lifetime, I have tried to embrace recovery and its lessons.
If I do not embrace recovery, I will have another lifetime of abuse
> because I did not learn what I came here to learn.

There is no escape from learning my lessons.
> I can choose to learn them in this lifetime or in the next.

But postponing will not change anything.
This belief has motivated me often to work hard and learn well.

To assist with learning major lessons this lifetime,
> we have consciously chosen aspects of this life.

These include:
> our physical characteristics,
> our emotional strengths and weaknesses,
> our mental abilities, our specific parents and family lines,
> our cultural, economic, social, religious,
> ethnic background.

Some may balk at this,
> choosing to believe God has made all these decisions.

That is, of course, a fine and acceptable theology.
However there are three reasons I do not believe this theology.

A. Each and every part of creation is part of the Divine.
We are not the totality of God, but Divine nonetheless.
So believing God chose all my characteristics or that I chose them
> is virtually one and the same
> > with categorically the same conclusion:
> > > I am fully responsible for my life, my lessons,
> > > and my soul tasks.

B. If I believe God has given me my lot in life,
    it is much easier to blame God for my struggles.

Using blame, I can abdicate responsibility for all my issues:
    my abusive childhood, my addictions, my poor eyesight,
    my broken relationships, my unhappiness.
Blaming God or someone else leaves me stuck
    in victim mentality and inertia.

C. Blaming others or being the victim keeps me from being an adult
    by shifting my attention.
If I can find someone else to focus on
    then I do not need to focus on myself or my issues.
Then I do not learn the lessons that I need to learn.

This in no way states that my parents do not have responsibility.
They came here to learn lessons also.
It is not my job [nor is it my business]
    to know if they learned their lessons.
My job is to learn mine.

The blueprint containing all our information about this lifetime
    is in the fifth chakra.[69]
The energetic mechanism is located on either side of the neck.
It resembles a three-pronged fork and holds all the information
    regarding this lifetime—
    our physical, emotional, mental, communal, spiritual data.

The first of the three prongs is located furthest outside the neck.
It contains information on propensity for health and illness,
    mannerisms and physical characteristics.
The second prong is where one's soul and body come together.
The top part of the prong is the site of the soul
    therefore usually lighter in energy.
The bottom part is the place of the body,
    usually darker or heavier in energy.

This second prong contains information
    regarding why you chose this body:
    these genes, goals of the soul,
        areas that the soul needs to be mindful regarding body,
        areas that the body needs to be mindful regarding soul,
        reasons why you chose your family and friends.

The third prong is the inner prong.
This is where the soul has it's privacy and solitude.
If privacy was lost due to abuse, one can rebuild it.

One can read the prongs and learn much about
    the purpose of this lifetime.
It can give clarity to motives as well as circumstances.

---

[69] Bergeson.

3. Intuitive Abilities
The fifth chakra is the site where we receive and send information
        from both the physical and spiritual worlds.
When one is sensitive to the energetic world, one is being intuitive.
Every human is intuitive—
        it's our birthright
         and each person can develop
          their intuitive abilities with practice.

Although intuition is governed in the sixth chakra
        we receive information through our fifth.
There are several ways to be intuitive in the human body;
        one is not better than another, just different.
Each person's task is to discern how he or she is sensitive to energy
        and work to develop that ability.

Clairaudience literally means "clear hearing".
        One is sensitive to energy and information
          through hearing.
Clairvoyance literally means "clear seeing".
        One sees energy and receives information visually.

Clairsentience literally means "clear knowing".
        One has the sense of knowing what is real and true.
Kinesthetic means one's physical body is sensitive to energy.
        One feels the energy in the "gut" or in the heart.

Telepathy is the general term for energetic communication.
Anodea Judith describes it as the art of hearing
        the whispers of another across even great distances.[70]
Telepathy requires us to be still
        to turn off the racings of our minds, to listen and hear.

Broadband telepathy is the ability to pick up distant information.
This information may be about a single event
        such as an earthquake in Alaska
          when one is in Minnesota,
Or this information may be about a collective group energy
        such as being sensitive to the energy of people
          in that quake.

Narrowband telepathy is energetically connecting from a distance
        to individuals or smaller groups of people
        and being sensitive to their particular situation.
For example, I might be imitatively aware of a family member's crisis
when she is in the Alaska earthquake
        and I am in Minnesota.

Transmediumship is the ability to channel other beings.
Translated as "intuitive speaking", being a transmedium means
        you have the ability to allow another being
          to use your body:
            your voice, hands, feet, or entire physical body.
Because you are senior in your space, you decide if and when
        you will use this ability to channel another being.
Reasons for channeling another being would include:
        assistance with specific actions, teaching, healing.

---

[70] Judith, 291.

One example of tranmediumship happened on a trip to Ireland.
My partner Beth and I rented a car for sightseeing.

Being concerned about driving on the opposite side of the road
    Beth asked for a spiritual helper to aid in driving.
She got help from a little old Irishman to help navigate;
    he drove the car through her hands.

Not all persons are transmedium.
It requires a specific circuitry—
    one may or may not have this type of energetic system.
See Read for Imation Abilities in the 5th Practices section for more.

5th Synopsis
Truthful communication and interaction is vital to the chakra's health.
When the fifth is too closed, I am silent when I need to speak.
    When it is too open, I speak when I need to be silent.

When the fifth is blocked, my senses are dulled.
When I listen to others, I think of myself first.
When I speak, I choose to lie as a means to avoid the truth.

When I am balanced, I communicate effectively.
My senses are attuned to all creation.
Because I stand in my power
    I am able to hear another's truth with empathy
        and respond with compassion.
I speak my truth clearly and articulately,
    as well as listen to others with clarity and calm.

5th PRACTICES

Read the 5th Chakra
Read the strengths of the fifth chakra.
Read your throat.	What do you see? Hear? Feel? Know?
Read your mouth.	What do you see? Hear? Feel? Know?
Read your nose.	What do you see? Hear? Feel? Know?
Read your eyes.	What do you see? Hear? Feel? Know?
Read your ears.	What do you see? Hear? Feel? Know?

What are the strengths of your fifth chakra?
Celebrate the strengths and power of your fifth.

Read for the blocks in the fifth chakra.
Read your throat.	Gleam lessons from your blocks.
Read your mouth.	Gleam lessons from your blocks.
Read your nose.	Gleam lessons from your blocks.
Read your eyes.	Gleam lessons from your blocks.
Read your ears.	Gleam lessons from your blocks.
Do you perceive any pattern	Gleam lessons from them.

Lectio Divina   "Divine Reading"
Lectio Divina is an ancient Christian meditative prayer.
It is the practice of reading a short passage several times,
      giving the Divine an opportunity to speak to the heart.
Lectio Divina can be prayer individually or in small groups.

A. Read out loud this passage from Micah 6: 8.
    "God has told you what is good
    and what does God require of you.
    To act justly, to love tenderly,
    and to walk humbly with your God."

B. Ask the Divine to speak to your heart through this passage.
    Ask to be open to receiving.

C. Read the passage out loud again, slower this time.
    If in a group, have a different person do this reading.
    Listen to which words or phrases speak to you.
    Slowly repeat it to yourself
    allow the words to penetrate your body and soul.

D. Invite God in; listen for the Divine.
    Spend a few minutes in union with God.
E. If in a group, share your word or phrase and its meaning.
F. Repeat the passage one last time, slowly.
    If in a group, have a third person read it.
    Take your word or phrase with you throughout your day.

Read for Truth
Read for your openness and honesty in communicating.
In the past twenty-four hours, where have you avoided the truth?
What was your fear?
What was your motive?

Pay attention to where you feel truth or lies in your body.
We lie loudest when we lie to ourselves
    so evaluate your honesty to yourself.
Do you rationalize to minimize the truth?
Do you keep secrets disguised as privacy?
Make a commitment to speak your truth,
    trusting in your boundaries.
Practice this using the mirror.
State your truth to yourself; feel it, embrace it, know it.
Let your reflection bear witness to your authenticity.

Gibberish
One practice to help open the fifth chakra is to speak in gibberish.
Gibberish allows one to bypass language and the cognitive brain
    thereby providing an opportunity for freedom of speech.

Make sounds in gibberish for each chakra, one through seven.
You can do this alone or find others and do it as a group.
Then write in gibberish.
Share with another what you wrote by speaking gibberish.
Then translate to English what you wrote to speak your truth.

Read for Masks
Read for the masks you wear.
What people, places, or events prompt your wearing of a mask?
What are you trying to hide?
Are you willing to start to take the mask off?
    Why? Why not?
If so, create a plan how to accomplish this gently and efficiently.

Admit, Apologize, Amends
Continue to take a personal inventory.
On a daily basis, review your intentions, attitudes, and behaviors.
When you are wrong, promptly admit it.[71]
When you need to apologize, humbly do it.
When you need to make amends, thoroughly do it.

Analyze communication skills.
Review your listening skills.
Do you listen thoroughly to another
    without forming your own response?
Do you listen without judgment
    or wanting to control the other person?
Do you seek out others who will listen thoroughly to you?

Review your speaking skills.
With whom do you struggle to speak the truth?
Examine your motives.
Do others have difficulty speaking truth to you?
    Why? Why not?
Do you speak when necessary?
Do you speak with tact?
Do you speak with accuracy and eloquence?

---

[71] Alcoholics Anonymous, 59.

Practice Study
Read Exodus 20:11.
"In six days God made heaven and earth
      and rested on the seventh day.
Therefore God blessed Shabbat and sanctified it."

Judaism focuses on prohibiting "work" to create space for rest.
Generally speaking, "work" is defined in Judaism
      as the acquisition of something,
      or the increasing of wealth or power
      or altering the world in some fashion.
Rest is the obligation to be with family and friends
      and spend some time in study.[72]

How do these definitions challenge your definition of work and rest?
Where do family and friends fit in your life?
What is "work" for you?
What is "rest" for you?
Do you observe any rest on your "Sabbath"?

Read for Fluidity
Read for truth's fluidity and were truth changes.
Where do you attempt to possess truth?
How well do you accept the reality that truth changes?
How can you continue to embrace the fluidity of change?

Koens
Koens are Buddhist brainteasers that encourage one
      to wrestle with deeper truths.
Spend a few days with this koen:
      "If you see the Buddha on the road, kill him."

What do you think it means?
What is the deeper truth?
What does the Buddha represent?
Why does that need to be killed?
Why would a nonviolent tradition like Buddhism
      use such a violent koen?

The answer of course is not literal.
The road, the Buddha, and the killing, are symbolic.
The road is the path to Enlightenment or your path in life.
The Buddha is a teacher you meet on your way.
The killing is the release or detachment of your conceptions.
Whatever your perceptions of the Buddha or Enlightenment are kill that image.
This is a teaching regarding reality as an impermanent illusion.
Nothing is permanent or stable;
      we must not hold onto any perceptions—
      just keep seeking.

---

[72] Hayim Donon, To Be A Jew, (New York City, NY: Basic Books, 1972), 88-89.

Language Check
Pay attention to your use of language.
Do you use "I" statements?
If you use "you" statements to control or place blame, apologize.
Place your intention on changing your language.
Check for your use of words that exaggerate,
      such as "always" or "never".
Replace them with words like "frequently" or "often".
Check your motives for speaking ,
      especially when you are angry or hurt.
Are you in victim mentality?
Are you being manipulative?
Are you being forthright with the truth of how you feel?

Read for Intuitive Abilities
Review how you receive and send energy.
Are you clairaudience, hear energetically?
Are you clairvoyant, see generically?
Are you kinesthetic, feel truth in your body?
Are you clairsentient, just know truth?
How do you practice to improve your skill and ability?
Are you telepathic?
Do you have broadband abilities?
Do you have narrowband abilities?

Read to determine if you have the energetic circuitry
      for transmediumship.
Ground very well.
Keep an energetic space of twenty to thirty feet around you
      permit no other beings in your space.
Ask if you have circuitry.
If you do, see if it's open or closed.
If open, close it with intention
      by running your hand down your head and neck.
Ask what your body needs because of this ability.

Keep the circuitry closed
      until you consciously decide you need to open it.
It is a grave responsibility to be a transmedium.
You are sharing your space—
      physically, emotionally, mentally—with another being.
You are always fully responsible
      for your intentions, attitudes, and actions.
Therefore use transmeduimship ethically and consciously.

Shout Out
Pick one characteristic you want to increase in your life
      such as joy, peace, love, beauty, contentment, bliss,
            strength, courage, serenity; confidence, power, health.
Shout it out as loud as you can for one minute.
This helps open the fifth chakra
      while powerfully putting your intention in the world.

This is really fun with a group of people, especially youth.
They get to shout positively and yell as loud
        as they can without getting in trouble.

Read the Blueprint
Go in and listen to find blueprint prongs.
Read the first prong.
        What is the state of your health
        and the possibility of illness this lifetime?
Read the second prong.
        What are the goals of your soul?
Read the third prong.
        Experience the solitude of your soul.

Chanting the Chakras[73]
Each chakra has its own tone, vibration, sound.
Chant all the chakra sounds to strengthen your entire chakra system
        or one particular chakra sound
                when struggling with that chakra.

1st chakra	Uh as in huh
2nd chakra	Oo as in due
3rd chakra	Ah as in father
4th chakra	Ay as in play
5th chakra	Eee as in see
6th chakra	Mmm as in om
7th chakra	Ning as in sing

Rejoice in Good Fortune Practice[74]
This practice centers on rejoicing for another's good fortune.
That is often difficult for us because we may feel envious or lacking.

First rejoice in your own good fortune by saying out loud
        "I rejoice in my own good fortune."
Then rejoice in loved ones' good fortune by saying out loud
        "I rejoice in ____ good fortune."
Then rejoice in strangers' good fortune by saying out loud
        "I rejoice in ____ good fortune."
Then rejoice in a difficult person's or enemy's good fortune
        by saying out loud, "I rejoice in ____ good fortune."

Be attentive to your resistance.
What are the roots of your resistance?

Mantras on the Gifts of the 5th Chakra
A. Breathe in "balance"; breathe out "balance".
B. Breathe in "empowerment"; breathe out "tact".
C. Breathe in "honesty"; breathe out "truth"

---

[73] Judith.
[74] Pema Chodron, Session Seven 7.3, "Awakening Love", Jan 13 – Mar 6, 2011, audio tape, Sound Tunes, Gampo Abbey, Cape Breton, Nova Scotia, 2012.

5th GIFTS

1. When I commit to being open
    to the truth each day
    as it presents itself to me   I am truth.

2. When I communicate my identity
    and my authenticity   I am reality.

3. When I increase my awareness of
    when, how, and why
    I avoid the truth   I am reflective.

4. When I truly listen
    and hear others   I am empathic respect.

5. When I lie
    and promptly admit it   I am honesty.

6. When I open my senses
    to the wonders of all creation   I am reception.

7. When my fifth chakra is open
    with good boundaries   I am.

6. CLEAR INTUITION

PHILOSOPHY OF INTUITION

Intuition is one's sensitivity to energy.
The word "intuition" comes from the Latin verb "intueri"
        translated as "to look inside" or "to contemplate"[75].
One is intuitive to the truth that he/she feels or knows from within.

Intuition is the ability to acquire information or knowledge
        without the use of reason, logic, or outside sources.
One gathers information from the energy of an entity itself
        not from its physical presence or expression.
For example, I am sensitive to another's angry energy without using
        his/her facial expressions or verbal words as clues.
I read his or her energy.

Reading energy goes beyond the senses and the analytical mind
        to the realm of essence and spirit.
This is inner perception: the knowing of truth
        that originates from within each individual being.
Possessed by all creation, humans see, hear, or feel the energy
        from other persons, animals, objects, space,
        spiritual entities.

Intuition is akin to having muscles.
 We all have muscles;
        some of us are capable of developing them
        more than others.[76]
Just like muscles, intuition must be developed and exercised.
One type of intuition is not better than another,
        just different because each body is different.
As outlined in chapter five
        each physical body will be attuned to energy
        in its own way.

All human beings are intuitive—it is a birthright.
The motivation for developing one's intuition
        is always self-discovery.
We are on this planet to learn who we are and why we are here.
That goal has many different names:
        consciousness, salvation, union with the Divine,
        wholeness, self-realization, adulthood, self-fulfillment.
However we name it, we seek to be fully alive human persons.
For our benefit, everything and everyone in my life is present
        to aid me in my goal of self-discovery.
Everything teaches me to integrate all aspects of my being
        as I work to achieve adulthood.

Therefore throughout life, I learn how to:
        care for my physical body,
        continue education to broaden my mind,
        develop relationships to open my heart,
        and learn how to be intuitive to listen to my soul and truth.
Because every single entity in creation is part of the Divine,
        the essence of every single entity in creation is truth.

---

[75] Carlin Flora. "Gut Almighty". Psychology Today, Vol 40. Issue 3: 68-75, 2007.
[76] Mahutchin.

Nothing can exist outside of truth.
Yes, we can lie but lies are fictional products of our minds;
        lies are not our essence.
When we read energy,
        we are reading an entity's truth at that particular moment.

Intuition is conscious contact with
        and integration of our entire being:
        physical, emotional, mental, and spiritual.
As we increase our sensitivity to the energy of our physical body,
        we hear and understand our emotional state
        in a deeper way
        because those emotions are stored in our body's cells.
As we feel our emotions, we use the abilities of the body
        to constructively express them
        and then use the power of the mind
        to understand their impact
        taming the mind so that unhelpful thoughts
        are transformed.
As we train our minds to focus on the present and slow down
        we connect to our spiritual energy.
As we increase our sensitivity to the spiritual realm
        we find our identity and our purpose.
We then can use all aspects of our being to create our authentic self
        and accomplish our goals for this life.

Wow! What an order!
Here's an example to remind you this is about progress,
        not perfection.
For most of my life I could not get angry.
My abusive past made anger too scary, so I shut if off completely.
As I worked in therapy to find my power and voice,
        my anger started to surface.

Once acknowledged, the rage stored in my cells demanded a heathy outlet.
So I compiled a list of all the ways to get angry in a healthy manner
        playing with all of them until I found my favorite—
        the punch bag.
I let myself get as furious as I wanted to release
        my deeply buried rage
        and for a long time that was cathartic.
But as I grew spiritually and worked on my intuition,
        I came to realize the next step was
        the re-training of my mind.
I did not want to be angry all the time or even most of the time.
I did not want rage to be my reaction when the light turned red
        or someone was rude to me.

Today, using my intuition helps me uncover
        the roots of anger, fear, or pain
        and helps me act in the world
        as an integrated human being.
My goal this lifetime is to recover from abuse not remain the victim
        to be an adult rather than react like a child.

Chakra work is the breadth and depth of integration
        for the human person:
        inviting symmetry of one's body, heart, mind, and soul;

integrating the individual self with the whole of creation;
and perpetual in its lessons,
no matter one's age or abilities.

The Warning Label
Intuition is reading truth.
However, being intuitive is an art and a craft, not an exact science.
The paradox is intuition is a complex simplicity.

As you open up to receive information regarding yourself,
    you will be more sensitive to other energies.
This demands your increased responsibility and accountability.
Your first responsibility is to your safety
    by maintaining clear and effective boundaries
    in all chakras.
This includes grounding often, consciously being present,
    being senior in your space,
    determining what energies are present,
    and asking energies to leave when necessary.

Your next responsibility is to others.
You may receive information about another without their request.
For example, at a faculty workshop
    I energetically saw a wound in the speaker's third chakra.

Ethically, I am duty-bound to do nothing with this information.
Since I was not asked to read
    it was not ethical to read another's energy
    without consent.
That's akin to walking into someone's house without knocking.
Nor is it my business to disclose information
    without the other's permission.
That's akin to sharing someone's secrets without permission.
It is my responsibility to set both energetic and physical boundaries
    in order to maintain morality and privacy.

You may be asked to read another's chakra.
    [See **Reading Others** in **8. Achieving Adulthood**.]
If asked, ethically share the information you received.
To that end, there are many warnings
    that need to be taken into account
    before using one's intuition in order
        to be ethical and helpful.
To explain these facets, I am using this example:
    I intuitively read that Mary is crying
    because her sister died.

A] My intuition is correct.
When I phone Mary, she is indeed crying
    because her sister just died.

B] My intuition is correct but not for today.
Sometimes what we see or hear or know is from a past
    or a future event.
In the spiritual world, there is not time or space.
So be aware that what you perceive may not be occurring
    in the present.

Perhaps Mary's sister died five years ago
        and Mary's crying is a past event.
Perhaps Mary's sister is going to die in the future
        and Mary will be in grief,
            but this event has not happened yet.

This is an extremely important facet of intuition.
What we read may be a present, past, or future event.
If we ignore it, we hurt ourselves as well as others.

If I erroneously believe everything I see is truth today;
        I can get egotistical—
            believing I have all the answers and know all.
After all, I have information when people die!
Additionally, Mary may get freaked out or panic
        if I tell her news that is not helpful or truthful for her today.
She may get frustrated and blame me for all her worrying
        or not trust me because her sister is fine today.

Although I am not responsible for Mary's emotions,
        I am accountable for the ethical use of my intuition.
It is not ethical to report my perceptions as truth for today
        when in fact, they may not be.

C] Intuition does not predict the future.
When I read Mary's crying
        I may be reading what Mary
        is setting up to do in the future.
Perhaps Mary's sister is dying from cancer
        and Mary is anticipating the loss.
I am reading the energy that when her sister does die, Mary will cry.
But again that is a future event also—
        and one that may or may not happen.

There are a number of scenarios in which Mary's sister dies
        and Mary does not cry.
Perhaps Mary's sister suffers for years in a coma
            or with Alzheimer's;
            perhaps Mary did her crying when her sister was alive;
            perhaps Mary dies before her sister.
Because of free will, we can set things up
        and then events change what we have set up.

My intuition reveals what Mary is setting up to do in the future,
        but she can alter her future any time she chooses.
My intuition of Mary crying is truth;
        I just don't know when or if it will unfold.

D] I am projecting my grief onto Mary.
For any number of reasons, I am in denial about my own need to cry
        so I read my issues as Mary's issues.
I am the one who is crying and use Mary as a means of avoidance.
Obviously not healthy or helpful for either of us.

This is common in both our outer world of relationships
        as well as in our inner world of intuition.
One must always be aware of this type of transference occurring.
Whatever we deny will work to get expressed somehow

and usually it comes out sideways—
at the wrong time to the wrong person in the wrong place.

Being grounded, conscious, and continually self-reflective
reduce the possibility of projection.

E] I don't receive the totality of the truth.
Because I am in a body, I am limited in my ability to comprehend
the totality of reality.
I do not possess the depth of understanding
for the intricacies and complexities
of how the world unfolds.

So I may read the energy that Mary is crying
but may not know the reality behind the tears.
Perhaps Mary's grief is the loss of her sister;
perhaps her grief is because
Mary and her sister were estranged;
perhaps her sister was abusive and Mary's tears
are not grief at all.

I do not know the whole truth about Mary's tears.
A vital fact about being human is I am limited;
I do not know the totality of reality or truth.

Adulthood demands ethical intention as well as action.
Using intuition is a birthright, gift, and responsibility.
Embracing intuition invites a deeply committed partnership
to the Divine.

Contemplation

I use the word "contemplation" to designate a particular aspect
of intuition.
Contemplation is experiencing the reality of Divine presence.
When we use our intuition to communicate with God,
we are in contemplation.

The intuitive person has had many names throughout history:
seer, psychic, medicine woman or man, guru,
dreamer, mystic, contemplative.
Whatever the word, the description is the same:
one who listens beyond words, sees
beyond physical reality
is deeply connected to the essence of the Divine.

Throughout most religions,
contemplation was the work of the mystic
the person who hears God's voice and responds.
Indeed that is the work of every single person on the planet
who desires adulthood.

In the words of Thomas Merton,
"My life is a listening.
God's is a speaking.
My salvation is to hear and respond."[77]

---

[77] Thomas Merton, Thoughts In Solitude (New York City, NY: NoonDay Press, 1986), 74.

Some of us may fear that the voice heard is not God's but a devil's.
Consider these aspects to quell any questions regarding the source.
Intuition always comes from within—
>it is the inner voice or knowing.

The world is often loud;
>the Divine is frequently quiet communicating in whispers.

The Divine is Truth
>therefore we may not want to hear what the Divine says
>but it will always correspond to our highest good.

You are always senior in your space; you can always say "no".

Certainly there are times when I misheard or misinterpreted
>the Divine and there have been countless times
>when I have let my ego or fear run amok.

I have been pursued by temptations and energy rogues.
>[Defined in **6th Practices**.]

But refusing to have a relationship with the Divine
>because of fear is not the path I choose.

Fear will not stop temptation from assaulting me
>only leave me less protected.

Fear will not help me define who I am
>just lead me in the opposite direction.

For me, the ultimate Reality is
>that a Power greater than myself exists
>and I choose to be in partnership with that Power.

This adventure is experienced in the mysticism of all traditions.
The Kabbalah, the book of Jewish mysticism, states:
>"The essence of Divinity is found in every single thing—
>nothing but it exists.
>Since it causes every thing to be,
>no thing can live by anything else....
>All existence is God."[78]

Hinduism's Gandhi believed "God is Truth and Truth is God".
Therefore our fundamental endeavor is
>the relentless pursuit of truth.

In every moment, with very breath, seeking truth is our quest.
And upon finding it, we come face to face with the Ultimate Reality.

The Islamic poet Kabir quipped,
>"If you want to know the truth, I will tell you the truth.
>Listen to the secret sound, the real sound,
>which is within you."[79]

The Buddhist nun Pema Chodron is succinct in her description
>of the Ultimate Reality:
>"You are the sky—the rest is just weather."[80]

For many Native American Indian nations, connectedness is key.
Chief Seattle taught, "Humankind has not woven the web of life.
>We are but one thread within it.
>Whatever we do to the web, we do to ourselves.
>All things are bound together. All things connect."[81]

---

[78] The Essential Kabbalah, (New York City NY: Quality Paperback Books, 1995), 24.
[79] Kabir, Poet Seers, http://www.poetseers.org/the-poetseers/kabir/kabir-index/index.html (November 13, 2014).
[80] Pema Chodron, Pema Chodron Quotes, http://www.goodreads.com/author/quotes/8052.Pema_Ch_dr_n (November13, 2014).
[81] Chief Seattle Pearls of Wisdom, http://www.sapphyr.net/natam/quotes-nativeamerican.htm (November14, 2014).

Christianity's Catherine of Siena
        speaks of the sublime union with God.
        "In your light, You have made me know your truth.
        You are light beyond all light, who gives the mind's eye
        supernatural light in fullness and perfection.....
        When I look in the mirror
        show me myself in you and You in me."[82]

This is the quest of the spiritual seeker:
        to know at our core we are truth and wholeness,
        to be in union with the fullness and grace of Divinity,
        to be one with the One.

---

[82] Andrew Harvey, ed. Teachings of the Mystics, (Boston, MA: Shambala, (1998), 122.

6th FUNDAMENTALS

6th Chakra Basics

Location	From the forehead to the base of skull at the occipital ridge including brain and third eye [midpoint of forehead]
Color	Indigo
Religion	Hinduism
Governs	1. Intuition
	2. Cognitive thinking
	3. Inclusiveness
	4. Guides

1. Intuition is our sensitivity to energy

It is the inner perception where one learns
        to perceive the truth of energy.
The goal of intuition is to listen to myself
        to learn who I am and why I am here.

The realm of intuition is the non-physical level of energy
        the domain where time and space do not exist.
Because the sixth chakra vibrates at such a very high level
        [faster than speed of sound]
        it allows humans to perceive things beyond
        what the mind or body can identify easily.[83]
Hence we may see things in present, past, future
        or in other dimensions.

Intuition is a non-verbal, non-auditory
        non-rational method of communication.
We hear, see, feel, or know the truth of something by its energy.
This communication is invaluable in our growth as spiritual beings.
        Who am I as a spiritual being?
        What is my life's purpose?
        Who is God?
        Where is our relationship heading?
        What do I need from God?
        What does God need from me?
To comprehend the answers to all those questions
        I listen intuitively to my body and soul,
        to all those I interact with in the physical
        and spiritual worlds.
Before I was born, I chose this life and its lessons.
I made soul agreements with people to come into my life
        and help me learn these lessons.

Every person I encounter [beyond just saying "hello"]
        is honoring our soul agreement to aide me in some way.
That does not mean every person in my life teaches me
        in a helpful or healthy manner.
For example, my parents and I had soul agreements:
        they would be my parents;

---

[83] Bergeson.

        I would be their daughter this lifetime.
Those agreements taught me very difficult lessons—
        how to survive an abusive childhood,
        endure incredible pain,
        experience the depths of loneliness,
        know the longing to die.
Though we may wish to only have easy lessons
        and cozy soul agreements, we learn far more in adversity.

In fact, I dare to say we learn little when times are pleasant;
        difficult challenges are the only pathways to discovering
        our courage, strength, perseverance, and integrity.

It was only when I developed my intuition
        that I could grasp the need
        for my childhood and its lessons.
I learned who I am at my core—
        not a victim but a person of worth and wholeness.
When I read my parents' energy, I learned they were at their core—
        not evil devils
        but persons wounded and unconscious of their impact.
The more I practice being attuned to the energy world,
        the greater understanding I acquire
        regarding my life's events and purpose.

As we open up the sixth chakra
        we become more sensitive to the energy of others.
It is tempting to focus on what we read
        or perceive in those around us
        but then we miss the primary point of intuition—self-work.
It is always self-work.

When I am more curious in other people's energy or lessons
        I am not focused on my own.
In AA, we call this "taking another's inventory".
This behavior is usually distracting, unproductive, and egotistical;
        it is an indicator we are running away from ourselves.
If you realize your attention is focused on others
        ground and bring yourself back to consciousness.
Listen; in the quiet you will discover
        what you are trying to escape from.

As you progress in being intuitive and open your sixth chakra
        you will enhance your primary manner
        of receiving energy
        and may also develop other methods of sensitivity.

For example, if you perceive energy primarily through hearing
        as you enhance that gift, you may become more sensitive
        to seeing or feeling intuitively also.

Our intuitive abilities atrophy quickly without use
        so it is imperative to put them to use.
However you are sensitive to energy
        practicing by using your skills is imperative.

The Civil War
In chapter two, I wrote about Benedict
        living in a cave for three years
        and Abbot John's comment that in the cave
        it's just "you and your demons".
Funny thing about demons is that most of them are within me.
Mohandas Gandhi remarked
        "the only demons we should be fighting
        are the ones running around in our own hearts.
        And that is where all our battles should be fought."[84]

Indeed, humans all fight a civil war inside
        between temptation and resolve,
        between wants and needs,
        between the head and the heart,
        between body and soul,
        between taking the safe path
                and doing what we came here to do.
This civil war is a life-long battle
        won with persistence and determination.
It takes tenacity and courage to confront oneself
        for that is exactly what this civil war is—
        the encounter of fears and ego
        versus our authenticity and integrity.
When I get besieged by the temptation to eat ice cream
        I want immediate gratification.
My head makes all sorts of rationalizations,
        my body wants to escape
        and I want to take the safe path of being numb for a while.
How do I quell the temptation and choose my needs over my wants?
How do I act in my highest good?
To overcome the inner demons, I need to listen to my truth
        sometimes referred to as one's "gut"—
        the place where the body and soul agree.
When my chakras are open and functioning well
        I can easily discern my truth and make healthy decisions.
Every time I participate in my civil war, it is because
        one or more chakras are compromised.

With ice cream, it could be:

I am ungrounded	[first chakra],
unconscious	[second],
I feel afraid or bored	[second],
gave away my power	[third],
I damaged a relationship	[fourth],
was silent when I needed to speak	[fifth],
refused to hear or see	[sixth],
or I am ignoring the Divine	[seventh]

To end the civil war, I need to intuitively read my chakras,
        heal what is wounded
        so my body and soul are in agreement and work together.

When you stand grounded in consciousness
        your body and soul both seek your highest good.
Trust yourself and your intuition.
Know you are the only one who truly knows
        what you came here to do.
Others provide input and advice but you alone know your path.

---

[84] Gandhi, dir. Richard Attenborough, (1932, Columbia Pictures, DVD 2007).

Accept your mistakes as lessons.
Sometimes you will choose the easier path
        and neglect your higher good.
Recognize and admit it as soon as possible.
Learn something from this experience and move onward.

2. Cognitive Thinking
This is the mental or intellectual aspect of our brain.
It includes a multitude of functions:
        processing speed, visual and auditory processing,
        attention span, short-term and long-term memory,
        memory, logic and reasoning.

3. Inclusivity
The great gift of the sixth chakra is inclusivity.
Everything in creation is part of God;
        nothing can exist apart from God.
Because all creation is alive with intuition and insight
        everything is connected
        and everything is known by everything else.

The vast majority of the time, we may be unconscious of this reality.
But the realty exists nonetheless.
Through the sixth chakra we strive to bring inclusiveness
        into greater consciousness.

As we learn to trust our connectedness
        to both the physical and the spiritual realms,
        we walk in trust rather than fear,
        embrace unity, and comprehend beauty.
To this end, the sixth chakra motivates us
        to communicate accurately and eloquently.
It seeks expression that is both articulate and exquisite.

Part of the inclusivity of
        the sixth chakra is knowing how to create our lives.
Everything we create begins in the sixth with our knowing.
We know, then set our intention, dreaming, and vision on creating it.
All intentions begin in this chakra with dreaming and vision.
        and intentions need clarity
        and strength to be materialized.[85]
When we begin any project, it starts with knowing—
        having an idea of what we want to create.
Then we plan, using sound and feeling.

We consider how we feel about various aspects of this proposal
        and test out our proposal by asking for others' opinions.
We then structure the project in time and space.
When and where do we want this endeavor to be born?
Then we create.
Finally we ground our project,
        connecting and anchoring it to the earth.

---

[85] Bergeson.

Everything we build starts in the sixth chakra with our knowing.
We may not believe it but we intuitively know how
> to create lives that are healthy and whole.

4. Guides, Angels, Healers, Helpers
Earth energies, and the ancestors in the spiritual realm.
Just like the physical plane,
> there is all manner of assistance available to us if we wish.

A. Guides are spirits who do just that: guide.
Because they are not embodied, they have greater vision and depth.
They are mentors from the spiritual world.
Shortly after I began serious energetic studies
> I asked the Universe for a spiritual guide.

One day I was trading massages with a friend named June.
She was working on my arm, when she stopped and said,
> "There's a guy by the table.
> I don't know if he is here for you or for me."

I said, "Ask him."

June said, "He won't talk to me.
> But he looks Native American and he is wearing a top hat.
> So I'll just call him 'Topper'."

After going home, I sat outside and I could sense his presence.
I didn't see or hear him...just felt him in front of me to the left.
This went on for a couple of weeks;
> I would try to see him but could not.

I would ask him questions but he did not speak.
Finally, I began to hear his voice, distinct and low.

Over the years we have worked together,
> we have built a relationship of trust.

Just like relationships in the physical world
> partnerships with guides is a process
> of building cooperation, collaboration, and confidence.

Topper is a daily companion as my spirit guide.
 I seek his guidance on almost all decisions:
> spiritual, moral, emotional, relational, professional.

When we decided to incarnate in a human body for this lifetime
> each of us set up three to five guides to assist us.

We can make contact with them or not;
> we can keep our agreement or not.

Whatever our decision, we have guides ready and available.

B. Angels are spiritual beings who function like personal assistants.
They assist us in everyday matters.
 When I was young, I knew there were two angels
> helping me survive my childhood.

They provided me with protection, comfort, and companionship.

Many religions believe each person has at least one angel
> assigned to them.

Some believe we have more angels with us in our youth
> when we are more at risk
> and as we mature, our primary angel assists us.

C. Healers are spiritual beings who heal.
That does include being restored to physical health
> but often it is our emotional and spiritual wounds
> > that need tending.
Spiritual healers, having great vision and depth,
> offer us what we most require in healing.

D. Spiritual helpers are short or long term spiritual aides
> ready to assist in a variety of situations.
The story from chapter five of the Irishman driving our car in Ireland
> is an example of getting short-term assistance
> > from a spiritual helper.

E. Earth energies are assistants from Mother Earth.
They include four-legged, winged ones, creatures in the waters,
> astral energies, and Mother Earth herself.
These helpers can be short-term or walk with you for life.

F. The ancestors are all those who have walked a physical life
> on this planet.
We can ask for guidance from those who have gone before us.

Senior in your Space Revisited

As in the physical world, there is a multitude of expertise
> in the spiritual realm available to us
> > if we choose to utilize them.

Just like in the physical world, we are senior in our space.
You do not have to take any advice or suggestion from another,
> no matter what realm they are from.
Each person is in charge of his or her seniority.

Spiritual assistance is just like assistance in the physical world.
When I go to a medical appointment
> I have three options for action with the doctor's advice:

A. I can take his or her advice on getting well.
Because I am in charge of my body and my health,
> decisions are mine.
Most of the time, I will take the doctor's advice.
He/she has more knowledge in this area and I trust that expertise.
The same is true for spiritual guides: I trust Topper.

B. I can ignore the advice.
I will still have my health issue and will have to live with it.
I have the option do this with Topper's advice.
Spiritually speaking, I don't do this very often.
When I ignore a health issue
> the problem usually doesn't get better on its own.
Likewise, when I can ignore Topper's advice,
> my issues don't solve themselves
> > and life usually gets more difficult.

C. The third option is to get a second opinion.
I can get another guide or healer or helper.
Some relationships work out; some don't.
You are in charge of what you want and need
> and because you are in charge,
> > you can ask for other assistance.

Just as one might investigate doctors to find a good match
> one can interview spiritual beings
> > to determine compatibility.

Interview steps are:
A. Ground and set good boundaries.

B. Invite beings in for an interview.

C. Stand in Divine Light and bring it down in front of you.

D. Ask the being to stand in front of you in Divine Light.
> Neither human nor spiritual beings can lie in Divine Light.

E. Ask questions; have a dialogue; get to know each other.

F. Say "yes" if you want to work with this being
> or say "no and goodbye" to any energy you don't want.
> Remember you may ask any energy to leave at any point
> > in a relationship.

If that energy does not leave, you are agreeing to it on some level.
Ground again, clear your space, then ask it to leave again.

The Universe is a bountiful place and there is much help available—
> in both the physical and the spiritual realms

We just have to ask.
Regardless of who your mentors are, he bottom line is
> you are senior in your space and in charge of your life.

You are responsible for all decisions you make
> and all paths you take.

Energy Rogues

Every entity in creation has energy:
> humans, animals, planets, rocks.

Just as I can allow another's energy to enter my space
> there are pools of energies that roam looking for hosts.

Energy rogues are free floating collections of energy
> that at any time
> > feed off our own struggles.

Because they are energies that are parasitic,
> they always go against life.

Energy rogues are not emotions.
Emotions originate from within me and are my responses to events.
So fear, anger, grief, and confusion are not energy rogues
> even though they may feel huge
> and out-of-control at times.

Energy rogues come from outside of you; they are not your energy.

When a rogue has infiltrated your space
> you may feel you're possessed—
> > like the Biblical demons have taken over.

Caught in an invisible entanglement,
> you feel powerless to release yourself.

You are not of course completely powerless;
> you are always senior in your space
> and you can ask for Divine assistance.

But energy rogues can be very domineering

and often feel very familiar because you probably
grew up with this energy in your household.
Therefore they find us more willing targets.
The following are clues that an energy is a power rogue.
    You say there is no solution.
    You see an instant fix.
    Energy feels outside your body.
    You feel stuck or trapped.
    Energy feels heavy, intense, dense.
    You say "I can't" or "I quit".

These are many predominate energy rogues today.
I will highlight a few that plague many in American society.
A. Greed is the rogue that drives us to always want more
    and never be satisfied.
Greed, contrary to the first chakra's law of abundance,
    perpetuates an atmosphere of self-indulgent insecurity.

B. Despair is the energy rogue of giving up or quitting.
It lays claim to hopelessness.
People who live in despair are walking death:
    going through the motions but not engaging,
    living but not alive.

C. Victor/victim rogue plays on a compromised third chakra.
There is only dualism in this energy;
    one is either the victor or the victim
    which of course is not accurate or healthy.
This rogue seeks to keep us separated from our authentic power.
Other names for this rogue include:
    controllers, dictators, doormats.

D. Abuse and addiction are energy rogues with similar pedigrees.
Both are attempts to control something or someone
    and are reactions rather than responses.
Both are an outward denial of our emotions
    by focusing outside ourselves
    produce feelings of being out-of-control
    and an inability to stop our behavior.
Now certainly there is a biological/chemical component
    to the disease of alcoholism.
But there is also an energy rogue at play—
    one that promotes unconsciousness.

E. Lust is a rogue of misused sexual energy.
It thrives on using others as objects for immediate gratification.

F. Conformity is opposite of creativity and individuality.
This rogue plays on one's fears to shut down
    and silence one's authenticity.
It promotes the falsehood that one cannot survive outside the group.
A good example of an energy rogue is a mob.
An event occurs that ignites emotions of anger, grief, hatred, pain.
Individuals gather together and soon form a crowd.
The power rogue senses the emotional struggles
    and infiltrates the crowd
    with despair, victimhood, desire for control, or greed.

The crowd, unconscious of the rogue
> starts to buy into the rogue energy
> > which gives birth to a mob.
Mobs tend to be volatile, unstable, aggressive, violent.

When we get caught up in an energy rogue,
> we find that we do things we probably wouldn't do
> > if we were more conscious.

When we get caught up in a mob
> we may do things we would never do as an individual.

Energy rogues are dealt with in the same manner
> as any unwanted energy.

A. Ground.

B. Be conscious of energies you do not want
> or are not yours.

Stop.
Listen.
Ask yourself if your behavior is "normal" for you.

C. Identify the energy; name it.
Know it's not your energy but a collection of roaming energy.

D. Say "No/Goodbye" to it.
Do this without any emotion, such as anger or frustration.

E. Get determined.
 Assert your seniority in your space.
Delve into creativity, affinity, laughter
> to counterbalance power levels.

Call upon strength to come to your aid.

6th Synopsis

When my sixth chakra is compromised or blocked
> I refuse to be sensitive to energy.

It may feel safer or easier to use my head, rational and logical,
> rather than intuitive.

I deny and shut down my intuitive gifts.
Remember intuition atrophies quickly without use.
Refusing to see the inclusiveness of all that exists
> I withdraw and react with conceit or intolerance

When my sixth chakra is compromised
> I am more susceptible to energy rogues.

When my sixth chakra is balanced, I am sensitive to energy.
 I am open to my own truth,
> seeking help from the physical world
> > of four-legged, rocks, winged ones, waters,
>
> plants, stars, planets, Mother Earth
> > and the spiritual world of visions, spirits, guides, helpers.

I seek to deepen my partnership
> with the Divine through contemplation.

6th PRACTICES

Read the sixth Chakra
Read the strengths of the sixth chakra.
Read your skull.　　　　　　What do you see? Hear? Feel? Know?
Read your brain.　　　　　　What do you see? Hear? Feel? Know?
Read your third eye.　　　　What do you see? Hear? Feel? Know?
What are the strengths of your sixth chakra?
Celebrate the strengths and power of your sixth.

Read for the blocks in the sixth chakra.
Read your skull.　　　　　　Gleam lessons from your blocks.
Read your brain.　　　　　　Gleam lessons from your blocks.
Read your third eye.　　　　Gleam lessons from your blocks.
Do you perceive any patterns?　　Gleam lessons from them.

Read Your Intuition
Read for your intuition and your willingness
　　　　　to be open to your intuition.
Where do you accept your intuition?
　　　　　How does your intuition aid you?
Where do you struggle to trust your intuition?
　　　　　What is your fear?

Read for Guides
Read for angels, helpers, healers, guides.
Who is assisting you from the physical world?
Who is assisting you from the spiritual world?
Have you been grateful for help?

Read for Earth energies and ancestors.
Are you asking for assistance?
　　　　　What is your resistance?
Are you open to receiving assistance?
　　　　　What is your resistance?
Who is assisting you?
　　　　　What other energies could help you?

Read for Inclusivity
Read for the level of your inclusivity.
Do you embrace your connectedness to all that exists?
Do you trust your connectedness to all that exists?

Improve Contact
Seek, through prayer and meditation,
　　　　　to improve your conscious contact with God.[86]
Practice whatever works for you;
Adjust or modify any practices so that it fits your needs to further your contact.
Listen, experiment, go deeper.

---

[86] Alcoholics Anonymous, 59.

Read for Contemplation
Read for your connectedness to the Divine.
>Do you embrace your mysticism?

How often and in what ways do you build
>your partnership with the Divine?

What are your fears regarding contemplation?
>What do you need to do to overcome them?

What questions do you have today for the Divine?
>Are you open to the answers?

What is your response to the Divine today?
>Are you willing to surrender?

Read for Energy Rogues
Read for any energy rogues in your space.
Are you indulging in greed?
Are you despairing?
Where do you play the "victim"?
Are you indulging in lust filled behavior?
Do you abuse yourself or others?
Do others abuse you?
Do you seek to conform to any groups?

Examine any rogue energies in your space.
Where did you pick them up?
Why are they attaching to you?

Examine any connections to your childhood.
Release all energy rogues you find
>and reset your intentions to be senior in your own space.

Chants
A. Chant "OM" "That Though Art [sacred sound of God.]
B. Chant "Sat Nam"[87] "Truth is my identity."

Read for Time and Silence
Read for time spent in contemplation.
How much time do you spend in silence?
>Where can you lengthen this time?

Evaluate the quality of your contemplation.
>How can you increase it?

Name your major distractions to contemplation.
>Which are necessary and which are not?

How can you reduce the unnecessary ones?

Tapping[88]
The body is governed by energy meridians.
Tapping on various points of these energy routes helps
>to re-balance and taransform.

Repeating a mantro helps re-program the brain.
Creat yor own mantras acknowledging the pain or fear you feel
>and the goal you desire,
>>uch as "Even though I am afraid of becoming alone,
>>>I live in abundance."

---

[87] Khalsa & O'Keefe, 59.
[88] http://www.thetappingsolution.com/ (February 9, 2016).

Use three or four finger to gently tap the following locations
Tap on the side of hand, repeating.
Tap just above the eye brows.
Tap the side of the eye at the bone.
Tap under the eyes.
Tap under the nose.
Tap under lips.
Tap one inch below and out from the clavicle.
Tap under armpit at the bra line.
Tap the top of head.

Read Lifetime Vision
Read for your vision for this life.
First Chakra
    Who are you?
    Why are you here?
    Why did you choose your physical abilities?
    Your mental abilities?
    Why did you choose your parents?
    Your place and time of birth?

Second Chakra
    Why did you choose the creative abilites you have?
    If you have children, why did you have them?
        If not, why not?
    What lessons are they teaching you?

Third Chakra
    What lessons of power are you wrestling with this lifetime?
    What is your lesson when you abdicate your power?
    What is your lesson wehn you dominate power?

Fourth Chakra
    Who has loved you?
    Who has refused to love you?
    What relationships are you building?
    What relationships are you releasing?

Fifth Chakra
    Why did you choose your gifts of communication?
    How does the strength of your voise serve you?
    How does the strength of your listening serve you?

Sixth Chakra
    Why did you choose your intuitive abilitiess?
    How can you deepen them?

Seventh Chakra
    What are you chief learnings this lifetime?
    What soul tasks do youhave?

Color Meditation[89]

In a meditative position, visual a bright disk of white light
        directly above your head
        from which you can draw colors and energy.
From th disk, visual the color red
        pull it down through your seventh chakra
        through the spinal column
        and fill up your first chakra with red.
Embrace the strength, centeredness, and rejuvenation of the red.
Hold red for a few minutes.
Retain some of the red for the first chakra [perhaps seventy percent]
        then taking a deep breath, release the rest of the red
        down your grounding roots into the earth.

Visual orange, pull it down through your seventh chakra
        through your spinal column
        and fill up your second chakra.
Feel the creative energy of orange fill your being.
Retain the majority of the orange for your chakra.
Run the remainder down your grounding roots
        and with a deep breath, let it go.

Visual yellow, pull it down through your seventh chakra
        through your spinal column and fill up your third chakra.
Imagine golden power coming out of your body at your solar plexus
        with ray streaming into every part of your body.
[The third chakra is in charge of energy distribution in the body.
The rays visualize our sense of inner fire.]

Retain the majority of the yellow for your chakra.
Run the remainder down your grounding roots
        and with a deep breath, let it go.

Visual green, pull it down through your seventh chakra
        through your spinal column and fill up your fourth chakra.
Let the love and affinity of green wash over you
        embracing acceptance for yourself and all around you.
Retain most of the green for your chakra.
Run the remainder down your grounding roots
        and with a deep breath, let it go.

Visual blue, pull it down through your seventh chakra
        through your spinal column and fill up your fifth chakra.
Allow the blue to soothe and strengthen your fifth
        bringing clear, and truthful communications.
Retain most of the blue for your chakra.
Run the remainder down your grounding roots
        and with a deep breath, let it go.

Visual indigo, pull it down through your seventh chakra
        and fill up your sixth chakra.
Let the Indigo bathe your third eye
        and wash away any images that are not useful to you
        as it cleanses your inner screen.
Retain most of the indigo for your chakra.
Run the remainder down your grounding roots
        and with a deep breath, let it go.

---

[89] Judith, 327.

Visual purple, pull it down through your seventh chakra.
Feel this purple light crown your aura, energize
    and balance each chakra.
Retain most of the purple for your chakra.
Run the remainder down your grounding roots
    and with a deep breath, let it go.

Check all chakras to see if they are retaining their colors.
Colors you find comfortable indicate chakras in a healthier state.
Colors you find uncomfortable indicate
    perhaps a compromised chakra.
Pale, faded, weak colors indicate weak areas;
    vibrant colors indicate strength and health.

Offering Practice[90]

Offer appreciation and gratitude for all that you are and have.
Offer appreciation to all creation for something specific you value
    such as education, health care, loving family.
Offer gratitude for something specific you take for granted
    such as a furnace in winter or iced tea in the summer.
Offer appreciation for physical, emotional, mental,
    or spiritual presence of all creation.

Kitan Kriya Meditation[91]

Chant "Saa" [Infinity]
    while pressing the index fingertip to the thumb.
Chant "Taa" [Life]
    while pressing the middle fingertip to the thumb.
Chant "Naa" [Transformation]
    while pressing the ring fingertip to the thumb.
Chant "Maa" [Rebirth]
    while pressing the little fingertip to the thumb.

Mantras on the Gifts of the 6th Chakra

A. Breathe in "inclusiveness"; breathe out "appreciation".
B. Breathe in "trust"; breathe out "vision".
C. Breathe in "light"; breathe out "light".

---

[90] Pema Chodron, Session Seven 7.5, "Awakening Love", Jan 13 – Mar 6, 2011, audio tape, Sound Tunes, Gampo Abbey, Cape Breton, Nova Scotia, 2012.
[91] Harams Khalsa & Daryl O'Keeffe, The Kundalini Yoga Experience, (New York:: NY, Fireside Books, 2002), 62.

6th GIFTS

1. When I listen
     to my inner self   I am intuition.

2. When I am attuned
     to the Divine   I am contemplation.

3. When I embrace the
     inter-connectedness
     of all that exists
     in all creation   I am inclusivity.

4. When I ask and receive help
     from both the physical
     and spiritual worlds   I am inter-reliant.

5. When I stand in my knowing   I am light.

6. When I am in union
     with the Ultimate Reality   I am fulfillment.

7. When my sixth chakra is open
     with good boundaries   I am.

7. COMPLETE SURRENDER

PHILOSOPHY OF SURRENDER

Surrender is the conscious decision
    to turn over one's self to a Higher Power.
To submit to the Divine is the essence of spirituality
    and the ultimate conclusion of our relationship with the Divine.
Surrender is both the foundation and the summit of being an adult.

Surrender is the acceptance of one's position
    in the whole of creation.
I am a human being; as an embodied spirit,
    I have natural limitations.
My particular gifts and weakness are interwoven:
    intuitive yet very myopic eyes,
    an addictive personality balanced
        by a passion for recovery,
    a brain that loves puzzles
        but is not attuned to foreign languages or math,
    a body, though incredibly strong, can't dance.
The greatest limitation is this body, made of earth,
    will eventually deteriorate and die.
Even my soul, although part of the Divine, is limited:
    I am not the totality of God.

Accepting the realities of our humanity is the first part of surrender.
No matter how accomplished or successful we are
    the human being is a limited creation.
The second part is accepting the realities of Divinity—
    there is a Higher Power that is the totality of all that exists.
This Higher Power is akin to the ocean
    known yet mysterious, deep yet accessible,
    understood but still incomprehensible.
I am a drop of water
    not the totality of the ocean but part of it nonetheless.
In this life, I seek to surrender my drop of water
    into the ocean of God.
Though beyond our complete understanding
    this Ultimate Reality and all that is are One.
Therefore our quest in this human life is to surrender our very selves
    in order to experience the bliss of that Oneness.

All the synonyms for surrender speak to the depth of its importance.
Acceptance is to assent to things as they are
    without trying to change them.
Egolessness is eliminating the "I" in order to do the will of God.
Let go and let God is abandoning your desires
    to let the Divine work.
Letting go of the outcome means releasing the desire
    to control the result.
Relinquish means to remove the ego
    thereby permitting the Divine access.
Submit is to proclaim dependence on a Power greater that yourself.

Surrender means to renounce your ego
    and embrace a Power greater than yourself.

Turning it over is allowing your Higher Power to act.
Trust is the belief that all in unfolding as it should.
Yield means to allow a Power greater than yourself to take the lead

The Spectrum of Surrender
Surrendering to the Divine happens slowly, in layers.
While the goal of surrender is to completely yield to the Divine
        as humans with free will,
            we always have the option to surrender or not.
Indeed some people will not even enter the realm of surrender
        but live their lives relying on their own rational mind
        or ego to make decisions.
But if we are lucky, a challenge or crisis will befall us
        and we will find ourselves face to face
            with the gift of surrender.
The level to which we accept this gift
        determines the depth of our spiritual journey.

A. The first level is desperation surrender.
For most of us this first level comes when we are broken.
Life has dealt us a crushing blow
        and we are empty, lost, and broken into pieces.
One can be broken from
        addiction, abuse, depression, disease, illness, loss.
Being at the bottom, sucking silt off the floor
            leaves us little alternative—
        the choice is either surrender or die.
So we begrudgingly and reluctantly surrender to a Higher Power.
For me, this moment occurred the last time I got drunk.
In an attempt to escape the pain of my abusive childhood,
        I slit my wrists but couldn't cut deep enough.
I stood at the crossroads: broken, empty, and desperate.
I either had to get a lot better at suicide or begin recovery.

With our first despairing whispers of surrender
        what we discover is quite miraculous:
            our lives become manageable, we become sane.
Life does not get easier but it gets better
        as our Higher Power does for us
            what we could not do for ourselves.
This success motivates us to move to the next level.

B. Then second level is surrendering all defects.
We have let go of the objects that crippled us:
        alcohol or drugs, grief or loss, etc.

Now feeling such positive change from surrendering
        when we were empty and at the bottom
        we are willing to turn over all aspects of our life
        that cause us difficulty or pain
        in hopes of continued improvement.
So we let go of all our stumbling blocks—
        character defects and shortcomings
        that hinder our growth.

I was more than happy to surrender
        my defects of self-righteousness and egotism

        if it meant an increase in my happiness and maturity.
It was empowering and freeing to clean out harmful attributes
            of my personality through
            working my Twelve Step program
            and letting the Divine guide my life.
The results included God filling me with me
        with gratitude and acceptance.

C. Next is the level of selective surrender.
This is when, although we are willing to surrender all the stuff
            we don't want,
            we have really no intentions of letting go
            of the stuff we do want.

I am willing to give God my addictions, self-righteousness,
        abusive childhood, anger, and pain
        but am holding tight to my happiness, devoted family,
        security, home, status, food in the frig, respect,
        bank accounts, new car, tech gizmos, popularity.

Our fear in surrendering is that God will ask too much
        or take too much.
Our fallacy is thinking that by not surrendering,
        we can control the outcome.

This is the level of head over heart, of ego rather than submission.
Most of the time, this action is not nefarious;
        we just want what we want when we want it.
An example is my decision to go to graduate school.
I asked for Divine assistance in choosing graduate schools
        and was given three possibilities.

But here's where my selective surrender took over.
I immediately rejected one of the schools to concentrate
        on St. John's University in Collegeville, MN,
        and another university in the Twin Cities.

After investigating both, I chose St. John's over the other one
        based solely on the length of their Masters' programs:
        SJU was two years, the other one was three.
This was a rational, analytical, economic, thinking decision;
I did not consult God
        let alone submit to Divine will because I wanted St. John's.
I selectively yielded to the Divine in the beginning of this process;
        but refused to even consider surrender later on.
In other words, I surrendered only partial.

This level is quite alluring because we can rationalize
        our decisions very compellingly.
I don't have enough money for the other school
        so St. John's must be the "right" decision.
Having done my research, I know St. John's is the best place for me.
I've surrendered the biggest problems in my life, isn't that enough?
Don't I get to do what I want to do sometimes?

These first three levels of surrender are rooted in need—
        something is problematic and after trying everything else
        we then submit to God.

In the next level, we surrender, consciously, freely, and willingly
    all we have and all we are.

D. This level is complete surrender.
When we are ready, we surrender all:
    the things we don't want and all the things we love.
This is the heart of surrender—
    to let go of everything we worked for, fought for, cherish.
This includes security, home, bank account, loved ones, car, social
    status, health, hopes, dreams, security.
All that we have and all that we are is turned over to God.

If we persevere, we arrive at the essence of surrender.
As we live this level, we understand the true meaning
    and goal of surrender,
    of not holding anything back
    but fully allowing ourselves to be instruments of God.

All religious traditions herald the attributes of surrender.
Jesus speaks of surrender the night before his execution:
    'Not my will, but Yours be done." [Luke 22:42]
The word "Islam" literally means "to submit to Allah"
    and the word "Muslim" literally means
    "one who submits to Allah".

An interpretation of the Sinai covenant from Judaism reads:
    "Surrender and responsibility are inseparable attributes essential to every intimate relationship, including the relationship between G-d and humankind.
    We regard our relationship with G-d as a marriage....
    Jewish tradition describes the day that the commandments were given at Mt. Sinai as a wedding day.
    Mt. Sinai was held over our heads like a wedding canopy.
    The Ten Commandments were the marriage contract.
    Moses was the matchmaker.
    And heaven and earth were our witnesses.
    Then G-d said to us, "Surrender to me totally
        but be fully responsible for your morality.
    Submit to me completely
        but remain accountable for your actions."[92]

Hinduism philosophy states:
    wo things are necessary for the realization of God:
    faith and surrender.
    God has put you in the world.
    What can you do about it?
    Resign everything to the Divine.
    Surrender yourself at God's feet.[93]

Mother Teresa of Calcutta put it beautifully:
    "I am just a pencil in the hand of God."[94]

The essence of complete surrender is the art of doing God's will,
    of being in partnership with the Divine
    so that you are the invisible God in all actions.

---

[92] Chabbad.org, Surrender and Responsibility, http://www.chabad.org/library/article_cdo/aid/398912/jewish/Surrender-and-Responsibility.htm (November 24, 2014).
[93] Sri Sri Ramakrishna Quotes on Surrender, http://tapas-halder.blogspot.com/2012/09/sri-sri-ramakrishna-quotes-on-surrender.html (December 8, 2014).
[94] Mother Teresa of Calcutta, dir. Fabrizio Costa ugh, (2003, pro. Luca Bernabei).

The Will of God
The goal of this relationship is to do the will of God.
Surrender is the pathway to putting aside my ego
        and will to be the instrument of the Divine.
It means the Divine is the boss—
        I work for God.

My job is to listen and do what I am asked
        when I am asked to the best of my ability.
I am not in charge of anything but my part;
        the Divine is in control of all else.

Understanding why I need to do something
        or how it fits in the whole
        is not my concern trusting the Divine is.

Having grown up in a very abusive household, this was scary for me.
What if the will of God was destructive like my father's
        or manipulative like my mother's?

After much searching, I came to believe the will of God
        is always my highest good;
        my soul tasks and the will of God are synonymous.
My soul longs to fulfill the will of the Divine
        because that is why I am here.

It is easy to get overwhelmed by the magnitude of doing God's will.
Keep it simple: just do the next right thing.
Consider these as starters for your day.
        Today, what do You want me to accomplish?
        For today, what is the next right thing for me?
        What issues I need to address today?

Two ultimate conclusions can be drawn that speaks
        to the importance of surrender.
First, if indeed we are limited and if indeed the Divine is Wisdom,
        then the path of the ego is not in our best interests
        and being prudent, we would seek Divine assistance.
The second conclusion drawn is that if we are part of God
        then we are fulfilled only when we are one with the One, when we are united to the
Whole of Divinity.
Surrender then is fulfillment.

Letting Go of the Outcome
Surrender is very difficult
        because it demands we relinquish our control
As humans we are very reluctant to relinquish any control.
Nevertheless that is our challenge.
These scenarios help demonstrate the craftiness of ego
when we try to control the outcome.

A. I don't get what I want.
I have two eye diseases and have lost most of the sight
        in my right eye.
For years, I would pray and beg God for healing

so as not to lose any more eyesight.
Those prayers felt unanswered as each year my sight deteriorated.

As my anger and grief surface,
    I also noticed resentment and mistrust.
I blamed God for not helping me.
Never doubting God's power to intervene,
    I questioned Divine motives.
    Maybe God did not love me enough.
    Maybe I was not worthy of healing.
Struggling with these questions eroded my trust and confidence
    that my Higher Power and I were working together
    for my highest good.

Self-reflection taught me that when I don't get what I want
    or I get what I don't want,
    I blame whoever I think is responsible.
This is a frequent reaction of my wounded inner child
    who often felt unworthy of protection.
My little kid seeks two basic ingredients of a healthy childhood:
    love and security.
When she feels unwanted and abandoned, she blames others.

Using blame as a weapon is always the action of a wounded child.
Blame inevitably leads to victimization.
The world is against me; I am just a sad, helpless victim,
    abandoned by a God who doesn't care.

B. I get what I want but it is not what I need.
Sometimes we get so stuck on what we want
    that we don't even consider if it's what we need.
Although I have multiple examples from my addictive behaviors,
    this scenario focuses on my relationships.

I wanted to be in a committed relationship.
To that end, I pursued a woman who had obvious red flags
    that I chose to ignore.
After several years, the relationship ended.

I sought another partner
    and again chose someone with obvious red flags
    that I again chose to ignore
    because I wanted what I wanted.
This time the ending was a lot more expensive
    and a lot more painful.
Because I could not see past what I wanted,
    I had no clue of what I needed.
What I needed was to do some serious therapy
    in order to figure out who I was.
I kept looking for someone who would love me enough—
    what I needed was to love myself enough.
So I kept repeating the same pattern
    with the same increasingly frustrating results
    and the same glaringly painful lessons.

C. I get exactly what I want and it's exactly what I needed
    with invisible help from God.
Continuing the story from earlier in this chapter,

>   I chose to attend graduate school at St. John's School of Theology.
> But I did not see the invisible hand of the Divine working for me.
> My decision was based on the length
>   of a particular Master's program
>   which had two years of study rather than the usual three.
> The curious thing is that this particular Master's program
>   only lasted five years
>   those five years coinciding with my tenure at SJU.
>
> I believe the Divine worked through St. John's
>   providing me not only with a program
>   that fit my financial needs but my spiritual ones as well.
>
> So I chose St. John's thinking it was my decision;
>   God worked behind the scenes;
>   and I ended up exactly where I belonged.
>
> So everyone's happy, right? Yes but.
> Not acknowledging the invisible hand of the Divine
>   can easily increase my egotism.
> When I get what I want and it works out for my benefit
>   I can easily think I am smarter than I am
>   and easily believe I don't need God because I know best.
> This is dangerous for the spiritual seeker:
>   in forgetting our limitations,
>   we lose track of our higher good
>   in order to satisfy our primal or immediate wants.
>
> D. I don't get what I want but as life unfolds
>   I see not getting what I wanted is to my benefit.
> After three months of sobriety, my therapist asked me,
>   "Do you see alcoholism as a blessing yet?"
> I wanted to smack her.
> "Of course not. I don't see this as any blessing at all." I told her,
>   angry she would ask such an obviously dumb question.
> On the surface, there is no blessing in this condition:
>   no one wants to be an addict.
> I viewed my addiction like a plague upon my person—
>   I was a diseased, weak, pathetic, and hopeless outcast.
> In other words, I was stuck in self-pity.
> When we can't or won't look deeply into our situation
>   for its blessings or lessons
>   we can sink into self-pity, playing the mistreated victim.
>
> All of these scenarios speak of the pitfalls of trying
>   to control the outcome.
> The same scenarios can validate the gifts of surrendering control
>   and ultimately letting go of the outcome.
>
> A. I don't get what I want.
> Blame is a child's reaction; being responsible is an adult response.
> I am responsible to do what I need to do today.
> The question is always:
>   What is God's will for me today?
> My job is to do the next right thing and then let go of the outcome.
>
> So as difficult as it is, every day I take my eye medications
>   and give my eyesight to God.

I cannot control my eye diseases—
> I can only do what I can do today
>> and appreciate the sight I still have.

I have had to make peace with the reality
> that if I lose my ability to read or drive,
> that is the will of God and therein hold both
> the blessings and lessons that I need.

B. I get want I want but it is not what I need.
Getting what I want but not what I need is a detour off my path
> that I do not want to take.

Yes, I am human and often have to have lessons repeated.
But as soon as I am able, I need to learn my lessons
> and move forward.

An Autobiography in Five Short Chapters succinctly states this reality.
I. I walk down the street.
> There is a deep hole in the sidewalk.
> I fall in.
> I am lost; I am helpless.
> It isn't my fault.
> It takes me forever to get out.

II. I walk down the same street.
> There is a deep hole in the sidewalk.
> I pretend I don't see it.
> I fall in again.
> I can't believe I'm in the same place but it isn't my fault.
> It still takes a long time to get out.

III. I walk down the same street.
> There is a deep hole in the sidewalk.
> I see it there.
> I still fall in; it's a habit.
> My eyes are open.
> I know where I am. It's my fault.
> I get out immediately.

IV. I walk down the same street.
> There is a deep hole in the sidewalk.
> I walk around it.

V. I walk down another street.[95]

Pursuing women with obvious red flags was my "hole in the street"
> that I kept falling into.

Every time I fell down the same hole, I lost precious time.
I can make real progress this lifetime but time is always limited.

This scenario of getting what I want is the definition of insanity:
> doing the same thing over and over
> expecting different results.[96]

Self-reflection will awaken me to "the holes" I repetitively fall into
> realize I am repeating patterns I do not have to repeat,
> uncover whatever lessons are before me,
> motivate me to take a different street.

C. I get exactly what I want and it's exactly what I needed

---

[95] Portia Nelson, An Autobiography in Five Short Chapters, http://www.dwlz.com/Motivation/tips26.html (November 30, 2014).

[96] Brainy Quotes, http://www.brainyquote.com/quotes/quotes/a/alberteins133991.html (December 13, 2014).

with invisible help from God.
The reality is that this statement is always true.
Nothing happens without God;
    nothing occurs without Divine Energy.
Control is always an illusion.
Always.

It is always a mirage, appearing attractive and tempting,
    luring my ego into a sense of false empowerment.
Surrender acknowledges the Divine as the invisible Spirit
    of all that unfolds in all of creation.
That deepens our humility:
    we can let go of the outcome
    and trust that our Higher Power is always working with us.

So in hindsight, St. John's School of Theology was exactly
    what I needed.
It also happened that it was exactly what I wanted.
And my Higher Power orchestrated our match.

D. I don't get what I want but as life unfolds
    I see not getting what I wanted is to my benefit.
It took me three years before I got it—
    why my therapist viewed addiction as a blessing.
The blessing that addiction and recovery offer is self-discovery.
Without addiction and recovery, I would not have the depth
    of knowledge about who I am
        my strengths and weaknesses, gifts and talents.
I would not be the person I am today
    without the blessings of being an addict.

When we can let go of the outcome
    we get surprised by wonderfully, unexpected gifts—
    gifts we didn't know we wanted or needed.

This teaches a great paradox:
    everything that appears on the surface to be a hurdle
        may be a benefit in disguise
    and everything that appears to be a benefit on the surface
        may really be a hurdle.
My human limitations often obscure the truth
    regarding the situation.
Because I am finite, I don't comprehend the infinite interworking
    of all creation.
Surrendering the outcome allows me to trust
that all is unfolding according to Divine will.

How to Surrender
Surrender, like all spiritual practices, requires discipline.
Because of the difficult nature of surrender
    and the craftiness of our egos that crave escape
        discipline extends to all aspects of our being.

A. Discipline the body.
Spirituality promotes disciplining the body
    through prayer and fasting.
Prayer is a mandatory discipline of the spiritual life.
Despite the challenges, we pray regardless

of if it feels good or not, of if we want to or not,
of if we feel successful in our prayer or not.

I have used all the excuses:
    too busy and too bored, too tired, and too wild,
    feeling so abandoned by God that prayer was futile,
    and feeling so close to God that pray is unnecessary.
Sometimes I thought my prayers were unsuccessful because
    my attitude sucked, my faith dismal,
    my words inadequate, my surrender nonexistent.

What we feel doesn't matter; our words don't matter.
We pray.
And let go of the outcome.

Fasting is the art of self-sacrifice.
To fast means we consciously abstain from doing something
    that brings us pleasure.
The training to sacrifice what we want to do brings discipline
    and its rewards.

When we discipline the body our bodies get stronger
    and function better.
When I gave up alcohol, caffeine and carbs,
    my glucose levels balanced, my sleep improved,
    my attentiveness increased, my heart was happier.
Discipline for a healthier body also results in a healthier mind.

As we teach the body discipline in fasting
    we stand in solidarity with the millions who go hungry.
Because I have always had enough food,
    I can't comprehend the plight of the hungry.

Fasting exposes me through my very small experience
    to how many in the world feel daily.

It speaks to the incredible value of fasting
    that almost all religions promote it in some form.
Many Native Americans will fast during rituals like the Sun Dance.
Buddhism encourages the fasting of eating all meat.
Catholic Christians also abstain from eating meat
    during the season of Lent as a means of self-sacrifice.
Many Jews fast for twenty-six hours on Yom Kipper,
    the Day of Atonement.
Devout Hindus fast from eating any food one day each week.
One of Islam's Five Pillars is to fast during the month of Ramadan.
This means no food, water or bodily pleasures
    during daylight hours.
B. Discipline the heart.
Surrender brings forth very conflicting and powerful emotions.
We may feel two very opposite emotions at the same time.
When I left a very secure job, with great benefits,
    to start a new business, I felt unbridled joy because
      I was walking my path and I knew it deep in my core
    and overwhelming fear at no paycheck, no structure,
    no paid health insurance, no sick days.

When my business did not flourish as I wanted
    and the Divine asked me to further surrender

                my fear shifted to terror.
I had to discipline my heart's emotions through:
        finding healthy outlets for my fear,
        re-enforcing my commitment to let go of the outcome,
        consciously increasing my intention to trust the Divine,
        and daily committing myself to surrender.

Dealing with our emotions is a daily challenge
        of acknowledging feelings,
        expressing them in a healthy manner,
        then moving forward despite the trepidation.

C. Discipline the mind.
Surrender is not congruent with rationality.
Or with society.
The lure is extremely tempting:
        independent self-reliance so I can do what I want.
The spiritual path of surrender is the path
        of nonconformity with the world
            in order to be in a partnership with the Divine.
We work in the world
        but consciously choose to let go of the part of the world
            that indulges in ego, greed, popularity, escape,
                status, dishonesty, domination.
In fact when we walk a spiritual path, we will feel
        like a round peg in a square peg world.
It is seductive to quit and return to a more worldly path.
        Seductive yes, productive no.

Train your mind with these three steps.
a. Train your mind that the spiritual path is the way to wholeness.
If you have made it to this point
        some part of you already embraces this as truth.
Trust that you are more than your possessions or popularity or ego
        and know that you will be restless and unfulfilled
            until you walk your path.
Set your intentions.
Practice mantras.
Ask for help.
Trust in God.

b. Practice optimism.
The Divine is part of you; you can't get lost.
Trust that all you need will be provided
        and the most difficult lessons
            will have the most enlightening gifts.

There's a great story to demonstrate optimism.
Twin boys were opening their birthday presents.
The first unwrapped his box only to find a pile of manure.
He responded with anger and disgust.
The second twin unwrapped his box
        and also found a pile of manure.
He started shouting in joy and anticipation.
When asked why he was so excited, he responded,
            "I got a pony. I just haven't found it yet."

Optimism is the confidence that all will work out,
>   as planned for our greater good.
Yes horrific events will occur; we will endure great suffering.
But we do not have to be identified by our grief but by our strength;
>   our lives do not have to be measured by our pain
>   but by our recovery.

c. Encourage your mind to revel in the Mystery.
Despite the ego's crave for control, there is great freedom
>   in marveling at the wonders of the Divine.
Each day, appreciate the Mystery that is God.
Be in awe of your very being.
Pique your curiosity about the unfolding of life.
Revel in the surprises of the Divine.

D. Discipline the soul.
Because the soul's agenda is to complete all soul tasks this lifetime,
>   it pushes, prompts, propels us to action.
The soul frequently wants to move faster than the body.
Then the body gets scared;
>   we relapse into old behaviors or get paralyzed by fear.

Train the soul to be patient by listening to the body's needs,
>   responding to them with gentleness,
>   taking small steps, and celebrating successes often.

You are responsible for everything in life
>   that happens to you.
Everything!
Therefore progress depends on all parts—
>   the body, heart, mind, and soul—
>   working together.
Your soul knows the way;
>   train it to gently lead the body, inspire the mind,
>   embrace the heart with compassion.

Let God
The flip side of surrender is trust.
Trust is the act of knowing that your Higher Power is doing for you
>   exactly what you need, exactly when you need it,
>   and exactly how you need it.
And then embracing it.

When I was in graduate school at St. John's I had a class,
>   the title I don't remember
>   taught by a monk, whose name I don't remember.
But I remember this true story.
An older woman was having a difficult rehabilitation
>   after intensive chemo for cancer.
When my professor/monk came to visit her, she told him,
>   "All I can do is lie here and let God love me."

That is the invitation of surrender:
>   to lay down, be still, to be quiet, to let go, to just be—
>   and let the God of Compassion love us.

7th FUNDAMENTALS

7th Chakra Basics
Location   Extending from the crown of the head
                         to eighteen inches above head
Color   Purple
Governs   1. One's personal connection to the Divine
                         2. Soul
                         3. Knowing
                         4. Surrendering to the Divine

1. One's Personal Connection To The Divine
The seventh chakra is where one is connected to the Divine.
This connection is an intimately are essence—
        we are part of the Divine.
Gandhi articulated this very clearly:
        "We are all divine beings
        and our purpose is to discover our own divinity.
        Our outer self is body;
        our inner self is mind;
        our true self is divine soul."
The seventh chakra is the place of each person's
        uniquely individual connection to the Divine
        whatever we conceive God to be.
This is one's sacred space where each individual meets
        the Ultimate Reality.

There should be no outside interference
        from anyone or anything in this chakra.
When I was a spirituality student
        one of my classmates was completely unsuccessful
        at reading her chakra, being intuitive,
        or connecting to God.
She had been raised in a very strict Christian denomination
        that demanded blind obedience.
To that end,
        at her baptism,
        the religious leader put an "energetic cap"
        on her seventh which kept her a spiritual child
        by preventing her from accessing Divine energy
        and compelling her to use the leader
        as a mediator between herself and God.
There should be no mediators or intermediaries
        in our relationship to the Divine.
None.
Ever.
Not a partner or spouse; not a minister, rabbi, priest, pope;
        not a guru or teacher.
This is a hallowed partnership that each person must own,
        develop, and forge for him/herself.

If you discover a cap on your seventh,
        set your intention on removing it.
Say "No / Goodbye" with affinity
        to anything or anyone in the seventh chakra.
Check the impermeability of your boundaries
        ensuring the intimacy of this sacred relationship.

2. Soul

The soul is Divine spiritual energy the essence
        of the human being in this life.
All humans possess a soul, the spiritual aspect of our existence.
It is the soul that has taken this life,
        chosen characteristics and lessons.
It's the soul that inspires the body to be fully alive.

This is not dualism; both physical and spiritual aspects of humanity
        are necessary and valued.
We need bodies to experience life and emotion—
        souls do not experience emotion in the way our bodies do.
We need souls to guide us to our highest good—
        bodies struggle to be fearless.
Hence bodies and souls each have their own tasks to accomplish.
The body's work is pretty evident:
        grow and develop, dream and create,
        build and release relationships, learn how to live and die.
The soul's work is to motivate, guide,
        and challenge us to accomplish our purpose.
This effort is just as challenging as the body's
        but not nearly as noticeable.

As part of its work, the soul will leave the body
        through the seventh chakra to travel.
This is the reason grounding is the most important spiritual practice.
When the soul has been out traveling,
        we need to call ourselves home.
It is only when we are grounded and the soul is at home
        in the fourth chakra that we can be fully conscious.

Souls have tremendous mobility: they can stay close to the body,
        travel to any place on earth
        venture to new worlds or other dimensions.
The medical community has sought to provide a scientific reason
        for sleep but can find none.
Mystics know we sleep because that is the soul's time to work.
It is during sleep that our soul makes connections
        works on relationships and projects.

Sometimes we are unconscious of our soul leaving the body.
One common example is getting spun out at the grocery store
        as discussed in Chapter One.
A more serious example is from my abusive childhood.
When I was getting raped, my soul would leave my body
        and watch the event unfold
        from the tree tops of the family farm.

In psychological terms, this is disassociation.
An experience is so traumatic that out of self-protection
        one separates from the horror
        in the only manner available.
The mind and the soul leave the body to observe from further away.
The reason for this is to distance oneself from the pain and suffering;
        when the episode of abuse ends, one can associate again.
Mind, body, heart, soul can be reunited.

Sometimes we are very conscious of the soul traveling.
When I was on the Lake Michigan Car Ferry, my guide asked
    if I wanted to see Lake Michigan from the sky.
My soul left my body and we ascended straight up into the blue
        high enough that I could see
            both the Wisconsin and Michigan shores at the same time.
Then higher still until this huge lake looked
        like a small blue balloon.

As you advance in consciousness
    continue to ground whenever you feel out-of-balance.
Increase your awareness of your soul's adventures.
    When and where does your soul travel?
    Why?

3. Knowing

The seventh chakra is the place of the highest level of knowing.
Knowing, far beyond mere facts and figures,
    is our ability to understand
        not only our own consciousness but the entire Universe.
This is the place of enlightenment.
This is the chakra where no thinking occurs, just knowing—
    no doing, just being.
It is the least defined for the body
    the most difficult for us to rationally comprehend
        because it is most centered on soul work.
Being most abstract and the least formed in physical world
    developing the seventh is rooted in trust and surrender.

For most of human history, we have been drowning in information
    but starving for knowledge.[97]
Perhaps we have been afraid of the power of our own knowing.
Knowledge brings great freedom, influence, and responsibility
    and that terrifies most of us.
Adulthood is embracing of our knowing:
    knowing our identity, place and purpose
    both this lifetime and beyond.

This knowing is present in the outer ring of our aura,
    the energetic atmosphere that surrounds the body.
Each of us has an aura, consisting of bands of energy that highlight
    the strengths and weaknesses of our chakras
    and overall being.
Auras, approximately three feet from the body,
    can intuitively be seen as either
    chakra color-coordinated body outlines
    or as colored energy surrounding each individual chakra.

The outer ring of the aura contains a golden ring.
Through this ring, called the gold ring of truth,
    we have access to all knowledge.
This is the energy of truth, of divine guidance, wisdom, knowledge.

The gold ring of truth is the place of your greater self,
    your energy of consciousness.
It is the part of you that can translate the perfection of the Divinity;
    the portion of your being that is continually one with God.

---

[97] Judith, 377.

Sometimes called the Higher Self, the Real Self, or the Over Soul,
    it is the Self that you are in a state of becoming
        through your evolution
    through all of your experiences in time and space.
It holds all the information regarding our lives:
    past, present, and future.

Gold, the color of enlightenment, signifies this is highest truth.
Especially in Christianity, the gold ring of truth is
    artistically portrayed as a hallo
    representing the great spiritual depth
    of the person pictured.

4. Surrendering To The Divine

Surrendering to the Divine is the openness
    and willingness to let the Divine be in charge.
It asks us to turn over to the care of God
    all we are, all we do, all we have.

Surrender is an incredible act of courage:
    courage to relinquish control
    and courage to do God's will.
Our fear is either nothing happens
    or we are asked to do what we don't want to do.

A. Nothing happens.
We do what God asks but there is not movement.
In the spring of 2014, I left a secure job with great benefits
    to start my own business.
I felt like I was stepping off a cliff into the abyss of unknowing
    armed only with trust.
I knew at my core it was the right step but terrifying nonetheless.
I created classes and workshops, promoted my skills,
    launched what God asked me to build.
And nothing happened.
No call backs, few students, and little interest in my endeavor.

I was overwhelmed with fear.
    How will I pay my bills?
    Will I lose my house?
    What if I can't get another job?
    What will people say?

The fear was soon dwarfed by my self-doubt.
    Have I made a huge mistake?
    Did I mishear the Divine?
    Am I a failure?
    Has God abandoned me?

I prayed; I pleaded; I begged God for success of my business.
Nothing happened.
I prayed, begged, and pleaded some more—
    this time for help with advertising.
Still nothing.
And still more praying, begging, pleading—
    this time for understanding.
And then I remembered the tree.

Over twenty years ago I heard about the Chinese bamboo tree.
The story was a curious one
        and although I did not know why I would need to,
            I remembered it.
Often we tuck away memories that seem unimportant
        in order to access their wisdom later.

The Chinese Bamboo tree gives us a great education.
When this particular seed is planted, watered, and nurtured,
        nothing happens the first year; there
            are no signs of growth.
For the next four years, with regular fertilizing, tending,
        watering, and sunshine,
            this tree does not outwardly grow at all.
 Nothing happens.
After five years of regular maintenance, with nothing to show for it,
        the bamboo tree suddenly sprouts
            and grows seventy to ninety feet in just six weeks.

The tree was not dormant during those first five years.
It was creating an elaborate and powerful root system
        that would support
            both its growth and its place in the world.[98]

The moral of the Chinese Bamboo tree, of course, is patience.
Perhaps nothing is happening on the outside;
        perhaps much is happening beneath the surface.
On this case, I was working on
        roots of surrender, trust, egolessness.
Whether I will need in five years remains to be seen.
The point is that neither the timing nor the outcome is up to me.

B. The second possible outcome to surrendering to the Divine is
        we are asked to do something we don't want to do.
This is a given.
It's why surrender is so challenging.

In the spring of 2001,
        after serving my entire career in Catholic education, I quit.
I was burned-out and finished with both
        Catholic schools and the Catholic Church.
Three years later, my spiritual guide said to me,
        "You need to go back to the Church."
I did not hesitate. "No, I don't."
"Yes, you do." He said quietly.
I replied emphatically, "No, I don't."

Six months later I was hired by my old school to serve
        as a Campus Minister.
It was the last thing I wanted and exactly what I needed.
I was given the opportunity to learn how to
        create ritual and lead prayer for a thousand people,
          make amends to my Catholic community,
        and serve others beyond teaching.

What I have discovered is that when I surrender
        and do the things I do not want to do,
            I am astonished by the gifts I receive.

---

[98] The Chinese Bamboo Tree: Looking for Growth, http://www.merakoh.com/2013/07/09/the-chinese-bamboo-tree-looking-for-growth/ (December 11, 2014).

I revel in a deeper identity;
> marvel at the daily presence of my Higher Power;
> stand in awe of receiving exactly what I need,
> when I need it.

Life is still difficult.
It's meant to be because how often do we learn when life is easy?
I still struggle with fear; doubt, poor eyesight, addictions,
> and doing what I don't want to do.
But ultimately, surrendering to God fulfills me.
The path of surrender is the only path I seek because, bluntly put,
> without surrender I am empty.

The gifts of surrender are summed up in this insight:
> "Surrender yourself completely to God
> > and set aside all such things as fear and shame.
> Give up such feelings as,
> 'What will people think of me if I dance
> > in the ecstasy of God's holy name?"[99]

7th Synopsis

When the seventh chakra is compromised, I am lost.
Whether under-connected or unconnected to the Divine
> I rely on my rational mind or my ego to understand life
> which can lead to a narrow and limited viewpoint.

When the seventh is open
> build a healthy relationship with the Divine.
In partnership, we work together for my highest good this lifetime.

---

[99] Sri Sri Ramakrishna Quotes on Surrender, http://tapas-halder.blogspot.com/ 2012/09/sri-sri-ramakrishna-quotes-on-surrender.html (December 8, 2014).

7th PRACTICES

Read the Seventh Chaka
Read your seventh chakra.
Read the space from the crown to fifteen inches above your head.
What do you see? Hear? Feel? Know?
Read your aura.   What do you see? Hear? Feel? Know?
What are the strengths of your seventh chakra?
Celebrate the strengths and power of your seventh chakra.

Read the blocks in the seventh chakra.
Read the space from the crown to eighteen inches above your head.
         Gleam lessons from your blocks.
Read your aura.   Gleam lessons from your blocks.
What are the difficulties in your seventh chakra?
Do you perceive any patterns   Gleam lessons from them.

Bliss Mantras
A. Breathe in "In You"; breathe out "I rest".
B. Breathe in "We are"; breathe out "One".
C. Breath in "With You"; breathe out "I am".
D. Breathe in "In You"; breathe out "I trust".

Read for Surrender
Read your willingness to surrender all you are and all you have.
Where do you surrender willingly?
     Why is this easy for you?
Where are you resistant?
     Analyze your motives
What are you still holding on to?
     How can you let go?

Healing Work
Healing means to make whole.
  Go inside and work with your own truth about your woundedness
     and what you need to be healed.
Work with masculine and feminine Earth energy.
Work with your guides, healing beings and helpers.
Work with Christ Force Energy
     the earth healing energy Jesus brought to the earth

Straight and Crooked Arrows[100]
On separate small pieces of paper,
     write down your strengths [your straight arrows]
     and your weaknesses [your crooked arrows].
Using any chakra diagram
     place each piece of paper next to the appropriate chakra.
Notice which chakras have the most paper?   Why?
Which ones have the least?   Why?
What insights can you garner about yourself?

---

[100] Jones, 145.

Choose one of your crooked arrows to work on.
Using a poker chip, flat stone, Popsicle stick, cardboard, etc.
>   write two attributes that heal your crooked arrows.

For example on one side write "Balance" and on the other "Calm".
Carry it with you as a reminder of your intention and your goal.

Read Your Life's Journey
Review your life, the major joys and the major difficulties.
What have been your most important learnings?
Can you see how each situation helped you
>   to get to this moment in time?

How can that reality help you to further surrender to the Divine?
Where can you find the invisible hand of God directing your life?
How can that reality help you to further surrender to the Divine?

Spiritual Meditation
Ask Mother Earth to ground you.
>   You are part of Earth.

Ask for Earth's gifts today.
>   Revel in Earth's strength.

Ask the Divine to be in your heart.
>   You are part of Divinity.

Invite in the Wisdom of all.
>   Revel in God's Presence.

Consider the Whole of which you are a part.
>   You are a vital, integral, essential part of that Whole.

This is your place in the world.
>   You belong here.

This is your ground, in your completeness.
>   You were meant to be here.

This is you.
You are whole.

Play with Discipline
Read for disciplining the body.
>   Where do you need to self-sacrifice?
>   How do you need to fast?

Read for disciplining the heart.
>   Are you emotionally balanced?
>   Where is fear motivating you?

Read for disciplining the mind.
>   What old messages do you need to erase?
>   Practice optimism every day.

Read for disciplining the soul.
>   Do you get impatient with your progress?
>   Are you celebrating your successes?

Prayers of the Seven Chakras
Each chakra can be aligned with a particular day of the week
>   beginning with the day of the week
>   on which you were born.

For example, because I was born on a Monday

Mondays are dedicated to my first chakra,
Tuesdays my second, Wednesdays my third, etc.
Each day I set my intention on healing
and strengthening that particular chakra.

There are three options for this prayer.
Day One is the day of the week of your birth.

A. Prayer of Chakra Intention
Day One
May my first chakra be open so I may respect myself and all creation.

Day Two
May my second chakra be open so I may be fearless in my consciousness.

Day Three
May my third chakra be open so I stand in my power.

Day Four
May my fourth chakra be open so I love all creation with ruthless compassion.

Day Five
May my fifth chakra be open so I eloquently articulate my truth.

Day Six
May my sixth chakra be open so I am intuitively integrated with all that is.

Day Seven
May my seventh chakra be open so I and the Divine may be united as One.

B. Prayer of Chakra Strength
Day One
Today, may I be grounded in the secrets of Mother Earth.

Day Two
Today, may my consciousness be full and complete,
permeating every crevice of my entire being.

Day Three
Today may my power be marshmallow titanium:
gentle on the outside, steel on the inside.

Day Four
Today may my compassion know no bounds.

Day Five
Today may my communication bear witness to the truth.

Day Six
Today may my intuition illuminate my entire being.

Day Seven
Today may my connection to the Divine be bliss.

C. Prayer of Chakra Wonder
Day One
As I wear red today, may it remind me of the wonders of
creation and my link to Earth and Divinity.

Day Two
As I wear orange today, may it remind me of the wonders
of consciousness, the joy of being in the present.

Day Three
As I wear yellow today, may it remind me of the wonders of power
and ability to stand in my truth. without swaying .

Day Four
As I wear green today, may it remind me of the wonders of
compassion and know I am loved.

Day Five
As I wear blue today, may it remind me of the wonders of
communication and the integrity
of speaking and hearing truth.

Day Six
As I wear indigo today, may it remind me of the wonders
of intuition and the knowledge
that I am part of the Whole.

Day Seven
As I wear lavender today, may it remind me of the
wonders of surrender,
that surrender is the path to fulfillment.

Symbol Assistance
Read each chakra and discover a personal symbol
that corresponds with each chakra that speaks to you.
For example, a symbol of your first chakra might be iron, fire, dirt.
Use that symbol whenever your feel unconnected.

Practice Principles
Having had a spiritual awakening, commit to practicing:
authentic ground, fearless consciousness,
balancing power, ruthless compassion,
truthful communication, clear intuition,
and complete surrender, in all your affairs.[101]
Seek to be open and completely available to
whatever the Divine asks of you in all encounters.

Cradling Practice[102]
There will be temptations, trepidations, trials, and struggles.
When those things arise to confront you
practice the art of turning them over to the divine.
For example, when feelings of loneliness arise, name it.
Visualize the loneliness and turn it over to your Higher Power.
Let your Higher Power cradle it, envelop it with Light and Truth.

Read the Gold Ring of Truth
Read your gold ring of truth.
Visualize bringing your ring of truth down from top of your head
to the bottom of your feet.

---

[101] Alcoholics Anonymous, 59.
[102] Pema Chodron, Session Eight 8.3, "Awakening Love", Jan 13 –Mar 6, 2011, audio tape, Sound Tunes, Gampo Abbey, Cape Breton, Nova Scotia, 2012.

Move it up your spine.
At each chakra, remove any energies that are not helpful or healthy for you.
Ask any unresolved questions.
Ask for help with any issues.
Let the ring fall down to your shoulders
 and nestle around your heart.
Connect with compassion in your heart.
Ask what your body needs today and what your soul wants today.

The Surrender Prayer
O Divine Master, I give to You
 my possessions and my property,
  my safety and my security,
my addictions and my recovery,
 my health and my illness,
all who love me and all who refuse to love me
 my desires and my dreams,
my wants and my needs,
 my success and my defeats,
my work and my rest,
 my will and my goals
my body and my soul,
 my life and my death.   Amen.

Mantras on the Gifts of the 7th Chakra
A. Breathe in "surrender"; breathe out "bliss".
B. Breathe in "faith"; breathe out "healing".
C. Breathe in "gratitude"; breathe out "generosity".

7th GIFTS

1. When I submit to the will of God   I am surrender.

2. When I stand in my adulthood
    body, heart, mind, and soul   I am whole.

3. When I am in union
    with the Divine   I am joy.

4. When I use my gifts
    to heal the world   I am Divine will.

5. When I strive to fulfill
    the purpose I came here
    to fulfill   I am fulfillment.

6. When I become
    who I am meant to be   I am fully alive.

7. When all my chakras are open
    with good boundaries   I am.

8. ACHIEVING ADULTHOOD

GOING FORTH

Seven Words Going Forth
As you go forth in your quest to be a fully alive human person,
> may these seven words guide you on your journey.

1. Freedom
In 1986, I was struck by a wall hanging I saw
> while at a women's monastery.

Carved in wood were these words from the Gospel of St. Thomas:
> "If you bring forth what is within you,
> what you bring forth will save you.
> If you do not bring forth what is within you,
> what you do not bring forth will destroy you."

Bring forth what is within me—
> my authenticity, my integrity, my truth,
> my humanity, my Divinity—
> is my freedom, salvation and fulfillment.

When I do not bring forth all of that, I destroy myself—
> with fraud, deception, suffering, and isolation.

The freedom is always mine: the freedom to choose
> to work on my issues, to learn my lessons.

I possess ultimate freedom to determine who I become.

2. Authenticity
There's a traditional Jewish story that sums it up.
Rabbi Rubin was one of the great Hasidic masters.
As he lay on his death bed, his disciples gathered around him
> to hear his last words.

And the Rabbi said, "In the next world they will not ask of me,
> 'Why were you not Moses?'
> They will ask me,
> 'Why were you not Rubin?'"

Authenticity is being who we came here to be.
Authenticity is our identity.

3. Balance
I went to see an energy teacher to garner information
> regarding my future.

Feeling pretty confident in my energetic and spiritual health,
> I was totally dismayed when she began to point out
> my blocks and weaknesses.

Later, as I complained to my therapist
> she spoke with perspective saying,
> "Germ, there is always another block, another lesson."

We have finished the chakras but really we have just begun.
Life is unveiled in layers like on an onion;
> we learn the first level and move to the second.

There is always another level, another lesson.
We are always achieving adulthood
> always in the process of learning and discovery.

Strive to be an efficient student of your own life.
Embrace all adventures as self-work, welcoming each as a gift.

But don't get so absorbed on your work that you forget to rejoice.
Balance your life with play, gaiety, and joy.
Laugh, especially at yourself, often.
Celebrate your very being boldly and wildly.

4. Acceptance

In our humanness we want to believe that spiritual growth
> will make life easy.

We want relaxed lives,
> perhaps even fame, notoriety, success, comfort.

An ancient Chinese saying puts it all in perspective.
> "Before enlightenment,
> > chapping wood and drawing water.
>
> After enlightenment,
> > chopping wood and drawing water."[103]

Accept that being spiritual will make life better
> but not necessarily easier.

We will still have struggles, addictions, frustrations, and defeats.
But now we will also have wisdom, recoveries, triumphs, and joys.

5. Gratitude

Gratitude is the most healing emotion.
When we walk in gratefulness, we know peace.
Whatever your circumstance
> fill your body, heart, mind, and soul with gratitude.

No matter how difficult be thankful for your lessons.
Appreciate the splendor and wonder of all that exists.
Yes the world is full of pain
> but even with its sham, drudgery and broken dreams,
> > it is still a beautiful world.[104]

We strive to be happy and that happiness is rooted in gratitude.

6. Generosity
As you heal yourself, heal the world.
Give back; serve others.
You are not the savior with all the answers
> but a sacred warrior in the battle over yourself.

7. Blessings

Blessings to you in times of struggle and in times of joy.
Blessings to you when you are lost and when you are found.
Blessings to you when you are off your path
> and when you are on your path.

Blessings to you and your continuing journey.

---

[103] Judith, 400.
[104] Desiderata http://www.cs.columbia.edu/~gongsu/desiderata_textonly.html (December 16, 2014).

Service Prayer
The world is lost, guide it.
The world is wanting, fill it.
The world is lonely, embrace it.
The world is hungry, feed it.
The world is grieving, comfort it.
The world is struggling, teach it.
The world is wounded, heal it.

Going Forth Prayer
God of all creation, grant me
    courage to acknowledge and recognize my woundedness,
    strength to heal all the wounds I carry,
    compassion for the suffering of others,
    wisdom to use my power with integrity
    so I may be a force of healing the world.

THE ART OF READING OTHERS

The primary and fundamental purpose of reading
>is always self-work.

We are here to heal ourselves.
As we improve our skills are reading,
>we may be asked for our reading insights
>>to help others on their journey.

Preliminary Work Before Reading

It is a great honor and tremendous responsibility to be asked
>to read another's energy.

Undertake this endeavor seriously and ethically.
Like all work, reading requires practice.
Practice on friends or family who are aware you are practicing.

These are the steps to safe and ethical reading of energy
>for both you and the person you are reading,
>>the "readee".

A. Ethics come first.
Ethics demand that you only read another's energy with consent.
>It is unethical to read anther's energy without permission.

Reading is always for the readee's benefit, not the reader's.
>The focus is on his/her wants and needs,
>>not on your gifts or talents.

Ethical reading means you maintain strong boundaries
>so that the information you share is actually the readee's,
>>not a projection of your own issues.

As the reader of energy,
>always remember what you see could happen now,
>could have happened in the past,
>might happen in the future,
>or might never happen.

B. Review chakra locations, colors, and governance.
Make sure you thoroughly understand
>each chakra's fundamental elements.

C. Review your intention for reading
You read to receive useful and relevant information helpful
>to the person at this time.

Set your intention on being consciousness,
>with affinity, and in neutrality.

Be open to receiving and sharing strengths, growth areas,
>and possible solutions.

D. Reading is an art, not an exact science.
Always acknowledge free will.
You are reading what the readee is setting up
>and she/he may change it at any point.

E. Your choice of language is important:
    use language with eloquence and articulate.

Choose these:

might be	appears like	could be
might help if	looks like	possibly
compromised	difficulty	wounded

Avoid these:

must	should	have to
will do	need to	dysfunctional
closed	gapping hole	broken

The Reading

A. Set your boundaries.
Ground completely; put on your glass body,
    set your heart on affinity, stand in neutrality.
To maintain clear and effective boundaries
    between the person being read and yourself,
    put up an energetic screen for the readee
    to project his/her energy on.
This screen protects you from picking up the readee's issues
    and from you projecting your issues onto him or her.

This energetic screen needs to be clear, straight, and unwavering,
    placed halfway between you and the readee
    extending ten to twenty feet wide and from floor to ceiling.

This screen should not have curves or wrap
    around anything or anyone.
This serves as an effective blockade:
    energies stay on their own side of the screen.

The following introductory script highlights the key points
    to reading energy.
"I can only read what you want to share with me;
    this means that on some level
    you have chosen to share this information with me.

I act as a mirror to reflect back your issues;
    you have free will do to whatever you wish
    with this information.
What I read for you may be true in the present,
    might be from the past, might be an event in the future,
    or not come to pass at all.
You know your own truth; if anything does not ring true, it's not.
You may ask about, discard, or store any information
I will not discuss your reading with anyone else;
    nor will I remember your words after you leave."

B. Following the introduction, you will do the reading.
Reset your grounding, consciousness, affinity,
    and neutrality if needed.
Invite the person to speak out loud his/her first and last name
    or all their names.
Greet the person's soul or being with "Hello".
Repeat the name as often as you need to

in order to maintain clear connections.
Share with the readee the location, color,
       and governances of the first chakra.
Then ask, "May I read the first chakra?"

Share the information you receive from the first chakra
Articulate exactly what you perceive.
The images you receive may have different meanings
       to you and the readee.
By stating exactly what you receive,
       you allow the readee to get the information without bias.

After you state exactly what you perceive,
       you can add any editorial comments you feel might help.
For example, if I see a huge rainstorm in the readee's first,
       I say, "I see a huge rainstorm."
Then I might add, "To me, water indicates emotion.
       You may encounter a lot of emotion soon."

Although as a reader you can never be positive
       regarding the timing of an event;
       the closer the images are to body,
             the closer they are to this time and space.

Ask guides, helpers, the ancestors, earth creatures,
       and other beings for help.
Seek clarification:
       Is this literal or figurative?
       Past, present, future?
       Could I get more information?
       What is its value for today?
       What would be helpful?
       What are the lessons?

After you finish with the first chakra,
       say "I am finished reading the first chakra.
       May I read the second?"
Then share the location, color,
       and governances of the second chakra.

Continue through the chakras.
When you get to the fourth, you may also read for chords.
Ask the readee to state out loud
       the name of the significant relationship.
Then you may ask that person's being
       to show the relationship chord

At the sixth chakra, be very tentative and cautious.
The information is in the planning stages of development.
Use phrases like:
       One of the choices you're planning is....
       You seem to be leaning toward this option....

Ending the Reading
The final act is to end the reading and the session.
Ending is important—in both the physical and the spiritual realm.

A. After you finish reading the seventh
    state that you have read all the chakras.
Answer any questions about any information received
    or about the process of reading.
Then dissolve the screen and send it back to the earth.
Say to the readee, "If I see you in public, I will acknowledge you.
    But I will not remember your words
    or energy from this reading."

B. After the readee leaves your physical space, review your effort.
What went well in the reading?
Where did you encounter difficulties?
What do you need to change for the future?
What would yu do exactly the same?
If appropriate, ask the readee for feedback.

Double-check your ground and your boundaries.
Is any of the readee's energy remaining?
Have you picked up any other energies?
Clear and clean you space as needed.

THE GIFTS

1. When I am grounded,
    my body and soul are home   I am.

2. When I am conscious,
    I live in
    the present moment   I am.

3. When I stand in my power,
    I am authentic and powerful   I am.

4. When my heart is open
    with good boundaries
    I am ruthless compassion
     to those who love me
     and those who refuse
    to love me   I am.

5. When I commutate my truth
    I speak with tact
    and eloquence
    and listen with empathy
    and openness   I am.

6. When I use my intuition
    to heal myself
    I heal the world.   I am.

7. When I surrender to the Divine
    I reach my highest self   I am.

THE PROMISES OF ADULTHOOD

Adulthood promises wholeness:
        the integration of the body, heart, mind, and soul
        is the joy of being a fully alive human person.

Adulthood promises that all creation is cherished
        and respected as essential to the whole.

Adulthood promises conscious in every single moment
        to embrace the wonder of each moment.

Adulthood promises courage in the transformation of fear,
        acceptance of all lessons as self-work.

Adulthood promises strength as we walk in our power,
        perseverance in the face of conflict,
        bravery as we own our true selves.

Adulthood promises liberation from the mis-use of power:
        deliverance from abuse and violence
        deliverance from weakness and manipulation.

Adulthood promises that we have no enemies
        we see ourselves in all others.

Adulthood promises intimacy
        that we will be seen, known, respected, loved
        and receive that in return.

Adulthood means truth is embraced because we know
        truth is the essence of our identity.

Adulthood promises freedom—
        freedom from fear to trust
        freedom from conformity to authenticity.

Adulthood promises that surrender to the Divine
        is the path to serenity.

Adulthood promises the realization that we and Divine are One.

Adulthood promises that by willingly choosing
        the frightening uncertainty of growth
        over the safe misery of remaining broken,
        wholeness is ours.

Adulthood promises as we heal our own wounds
        we heal the wounds of the world.

SELECTED BIBLIOGRAPHY

Alcoholics Anonymous. New York: Alcoholics Anonymous World Services, 1976.

Anodea, Judith. Wheels of Life. St. Paul, MN: Llewellyn Worldwide, 1993.

Bergeson, Marie. Psychic Development Class. St. Paul, MN, 1998-1999.

Bisanz, Denise Hanna. Psychological Therapy Sessions. 2014.

Brainy Quotes. http://www.brainyquote.com/quotes/ quotes/a/alberteins133991.html December 13, 2014.

Caduto, Michael. Everyday Herbs in Spiritual Life. Woodstock, VT: Skylight Paths, 2007.

Chabbad.org, Surrender and Responsibility. org/library/articlecdo/aid/ 398912/ jewish /Surrender-and-Responsibility.htm November 24, 2014.

Chief Seattle. Pearls of Wisdom, http://www.sapphyr.net natam/quotes-nativeamerican. htm November 14, 2014.

The Chinese Bamboo Tree: Looking for Growth. http://www.merakoh.com /2013/07/ 09/the-chinese-bamboo-tree-looking-for-growth/ December 11, 2014.

Chodron, Pema. "Awakening Love", Jan 13 – Mar 6, 2011, audio tape, Sound Tunes, Gampo Abbey, Cape Breton, Nova Scotia, 2012.

Chodron, Pema. The Places That Scare You. Boston, MA: Shambhala, 2002.

Chodron, Pema. Pema Chodron Quotes. http://www. goodreads.com /author/ quotes/8052.Pema_Ch_dr_n November 3, 2014.

Desiderata. http://www.cs.columbia.edu/ ~gongsu/desiderata_textonly.html December 16, 2014.

Donon, Hayim. To Be A Jew. New York City, NY: Basic Books, 1972.

The Essential Kabbalah. New York City NY: Quality Paperback Books, 1995.

Flora. Carlin. "Gut Almighty". Psychology Today. Vol 40. Issue 3: 68-75, 2007.

Gandhi. dir. Richard Attenborough. 1982, Columbia Pictures, DVD, 2007.

Gandhi, Mohandas. Book of Prayers. Berkeley CA: Berkley Hill, 1999.

Gandhi, Mohandas. Essential Writings. Maryknoll, NY: Orbis Books, 2006.

Grenz, Stanley. Prayer: A Cry For The Kingdom. Grand Rapids, MI: Wm Erdmans Publishing, 2005.

Hahn, Thich Nhat. http://www.goodreads.com/ author/quotes/9074. Th_ch_Nh_t_H_nh December 12, 2014.

Harvey, Andrew ed. Teachings of the Mystics. Boston, MA: Shambala, 1998.

Jones, Blackwolf and Gina. Listen to the Drum. Salt Lake City, UT:L Commune-a-key Publishing, 1995.

Kabir. Poet Seers, http://www.poetseers.org/the-poetseers/kabir/kabir-index/ index.html November 13, 2014.

Khalsa, Dharam & O'Keefe, Dary. The Kundalini Yoga Experience. New York City: NY: Simon and Schuster, 2002.

Klassen, Abbot John. Lecture on Monastic History. St. John's University, Collegeville, MN. April 8, 2010.

Leech, Kenneth. True Prayer. Harrisburg, PA: Morehouse Publishing, 1995.

Mahutchin, Beth. Psychic Development Class. Minneapolis, MN. Fall, 1996.

Merton, Thomas. Thoughts In Solitude. New York City, NY: NoonDay Press, 1986.

Mohan, Mary. Conversation with author. Minneapolis, MN. June 1, 2015.

Mother Teresa of Calcutta. dir. Fabrizio Costa ugh. DVD, 2003.

Nelson, Portia. An Autobiography in Five Short Chapters. http://www.\dwlzcom/ Motivation/tips26.html November 30, 2014.

Rambam on Charity . http://www.jewishmag.com/ 60mag/charity/charity.htm December 5, 2014.

Ragir, Judith. Meditation Talk. Clouds In Water Zen Center, St. Paul, MN, June 1997.

Robinson, George. Essential Judaism. New York City, NY: Pocket Books, 2000.

Rowlett, Martha. Praying Together. Nashville, TN: Upper Room, 2002.

Sams, Jamie and Carson, David. Medicine Cards. New York City, NY: St. Martin's Press, 1999.

Sellner, Edward. Pilgrimage. Notre Dame, IN: Sorin Books, 352006.

Society for the Promotion of Buddhism. The Teachings of Buddha. Tokyo, Japan: Kosaido Printing Company, 1966.

Sri Sri Ramakrishna Quotes on Surrender. http://tapas-halder.blogspot.com/ 2012/09/sri-sri-ramakrishna-quotes-on-surrender.html Dec ember8, 2014.

Twelve Steps and Twelve Traditions. New York City, NY: AA Worldwide Services, 1981.

www.ingramcontent.com/pod-product-compliance
Lightning Source LLC
Chambersburg PA
CBHW050533300426
44113CB00012B/2081